SINS OF THE FATHER

THE SHADOWS WITHIN

VOL-II

BY

J OUTIS

Table of Contents

MOVING FORWARD

Prologue

A Letter to My Son

Dear Son,

As I write this, I think about the road I've traveled—the struggles, the failures, and the moments of triumph. Life hasn't been easy for me, and I know it won't always be easy for you. But the lessons I've learned, often through pain and hardship, are the greatest gifts I can offer you.

This book reflects those lessons—my failures, my regrets, and the wisdom I've gained in their aftermath. You are living in the light of my successes, the fruits of my perseverance. We don't need to dwell on those moments here; they speak for themselves. Instead, this book is about the other side of my journey—the darker moments that shaped me and, ultimately, led me to become the person I am today.

There's something else I want you to know, something I write here with a heavy but hopeful heart. Life has been a constant battle for me, and there are days when I fear I might lose the fight. I struggle with suicidal thoughts I wish I didn't have, but you are the light that keeps me moving forward. This book is my promise: no matter what happens, you will always have my love, lessons, and voice to guide you.

Every quote and every reflection you'll find here is a tool—a weapon to protect you when life gets hard, as it inevitably will. These words are here to help you face the storms with courage, find strength in your weakest moments, and grow through the challenges you encounter.

I want you to know that you can rise above whatever life throws your way. You are my greatest hope, my greatest pride, and my greatest lesson in love. As long as I live, my wish for you is simple: you become a better man than I ever was.

This is not just a book. It is a piece of me, a guide for you, and a promise that my voice will always be with you no matter where you go.

With all my heart,

Your Father

FOUNDATIONS OF

A FRACTURED

SOUL

Chapter 1:

A Childhood of Chaos

A Childhood of Chaos

"They say our earliest years shape us, but no one warns you what happens when those years are carved from pain."

I wasn't born in darkness, but it found me early. My childhood was never a time of innocent wonder—it was a battleground where I fought battles I didn't understand. The echoes of a broken home, the crushing weight of expectations I was too young to name, and the cold, unyielding grip of discipline embedded themselves in me like scars. These weren't brief moments of tension or occasional hardships; they were ceaseless waves, relentless and unyielding, eroding the foundation of my innocence.

I was born in the United States, a place that could have been home, but the world didn't stay still long enough for me to take root. My childhood was defined not by a single landscape but by a series of contrasting worlds that offered neither peace nor stability. From an early age, I became accustomed to drifting between them, a constant outsider in places that should have felt familiar.

For much of my early years, I found solace in Belize, a small country that felt like a breath of fresh air amid the chaos. The rhythm of life there was slower, more deliberate, and surrounded by nature's beauty. The lush forests, the endless expanse of green, and the vibrant local markets—all painted a picture of escape. The people spoke in a mix of Creole and Spanish, the languages themselves soothing, like an embrace that promised safety. Still, even amidst the serene beauty of Belize, there was an undercurrent of discomfort, a gnawing sense of displacement. It was as though the land itself whispered of some unresolved part of my life—an emotional rift I couldn't understand but deeply felt.

But then there was Hong Kong. A world entirely different. The neon lights, the constant hum of activity, the dense urban labyrinth that seemed to pulse with energy and promise. Hong Kong was everything Belize was not—vibrant, fast-paced, and driven. It was a city where opportunities were endless but also where expectations were suffocating. For a child like me, it wasn't just a city—a maze of confusion, a place where I never quite fit. I would walk the crowded streets, looking up at towering skyscrapers, and still feel small, like a foreign object in a place that wasn't built for me.

These contrasting worlds left an imprint on my heart. The constant movement between them did nothing but remind me that I didn't have a place to call home. I was a child who belonged everywhere and nowhere, a soul torn between two continents, neither of which could anchor me. The constant shifting between Belize's tranquillity and Hong Kong's intensity deepened my alienation. There was always something missing, something unresolved deep within me, and it followed no matter where I went.

It wasn't just the geographical dislocation that left me untethered. It was my family. The very people who were meant to offer me love and protection became the ones who shaped me into someone I couldn't recognize. My father, who should have been my pillar, instead taught me the language of pain. He wielded physical force, each blow marking punctuation in a sentence I couldn't understand. My mother's sharp words filled the spaces in between, each criticism cutting deeper than the last. The divorce was the final fracture in a family shattered by unspoken resentments. In the aftermath, I became the rope in their tug-of-war—caught between two broken souls, each too hurt and too lost to heal me.

The Silence of Survival

For the first four years of my life, I didn't speak. Silence became my refuge, my rebellion, and my defense mechanism. While others called it a delay, I now understand it was a survival instinct. I remained silent because my world felt too unpredictable and unsafe. In a home where love was conditional and emotions were volatile, silence was the only constant I could cling to. It was the only way I could make sense of the chaos.

Even when I eventually began to speak, I never spoke the truth. How could I give voice to the feelings that swirled within me when even my parents couldn't express theirs? The weight of their fractured love sat heavily on my tongue, and the words I did manage to form were like feeble attempts to patch the cracks in a house already falling apart. I quickly learned that in my home, the truth was not always welcomed—it could shatter fragile peace, expose raw wounds, and open old hurts. So I learned to lie, to tell small, comforting lies to smooth over the jagged edges of our lives.

I became adept at reading the room before I could read a book. I learned how to gauge the mood of my parents, teachers, and peers—how to shrink into the background when tension rose, speak when it was safe, and disappear when I wasn't wanted. Adults would later call me "observant," but I knew the truth: I was afraid. Fear, not wisdom, taught me how to navigate my world.

A Fragmented Identity

Living in Hong Kong added yet another layer to my already complex identity. With its bright lights and endless opportunities, the city felt like both a blessing and a curse. The pressure to succeed was relentless. The education system demanded nothing less than perfection, and the social fabric valued conformity above all else. But how could I fit in when I didn't know who I was?

I was caught between two identities: too "foreign" to be fully accepted by my classmates and too "local" to feel like an outsider in the West. My American upbringing made me stand out in ways I couldn't control, and my time in Belize left me with perspectives that didn't always translate in Hong Kong's fast-paced, results-driven world. I was a patchwork of cultures—none of them fit together seamlessly.

At school, I was neither the best nor the worst. I didn't stand out in any major way, but I wasn't invisible either. My strategy for survival was adaptability. I became a chameleon, blending into different social circles just enough to avoid scrutiny, but I lost pieces of myself in the process. I was trying to fit in everywhere while simultaneously losing the essence of who I was.

Emotional Repression

"When you don't feel safe to express your emotions, they don't disappear—they fester."

Emotions were never something I could express freely. At home, showing emotion was a weakness. Tears were dismissed with harsh words, anger was punished with even harsher discipline, and fear was treated like a trait of the weak. My father's lessons were clear: emotions were distractions, vulnerabilities that only made you more susceptible to harm.

So, I learned to bottle up my feelings, to shove them deep inside where they could fester quietly, like rotting fruit hidden in the back of the pantry. But emotions don't stay quiet forever. Eventually, they demand to be felt. And when they did surface, they came out with a vengeance—like an uncontrollable wave crashing over everything in its path. I would lash out in anger, break down in tears, or withdraw into myself completely. And every time, I felt ashamed not just for the outburst but for the emotions themselves.

To my son: Feel your emotions. They are not signs of weakness but vital parts of what makes you human. Do not fear them. The sooner you learn to understand and accept them, the stronger you will become.

The Birth of Personas

In my search for acceptance, I began to create masks. At first, they were harmless—just small adjustments to my personality here and there. But as I grew older, these small adjustments became full-fledged personas. Each one reflected a side of myself that I couldn't fully reconcile. The achiever, the joker, the rebel, the manipulator—each mask had a purpose, each serving as a shield against the world's judgment.

For my teachers, the achiever was a way to gain validation in a home where praise was rare. The joker was for my classmates, a way to deflect attention from the insecurities I carried. The rebel was for my parents, a silent protest against the expectations they heaped on me. The manipulator? He was the darkest side of me, the one who learned to bend situations to my will when I felt powerless.

It was too late when I realized that I had fragmented myself into different personas. These masks had become so ingrained in my identity that I no longer knew who I was beneath them. I was proud, angry, envious—all the sins I had come to accept as part of my personality. My personas shielded me from the world but also trapped me in a prison of my own making. I had become so adept at pretending that I lost sight of the truth. My talents, emotions, and relationships became tools to maintain the illusion of who I was.

Cultural Dissonance

"When caught between two worlds, neither feels like home."

Belize and Hong Kong were opposites. Belize was slow, peaceful, and community-oriented. Hong Kong was fast, competitive, and individualistic. Living between these two worlds left me feeling like I belonged in neither.

In Belize, I was the kid who had "seen the world," someone who could talk about life beyond the island's borders, but it set me apart. In Hong Kong, I was the foreigner, the outsider with a fluency in English but imperfect Cantonese. Adapting to each culture didn't mean I ever truly belonged to either. Belonging isn't just about fitting in—it's about being seen for who you are. And in both places, I was unseen, a shadow in the crowd, a stranger in my own life.

To my son: Embrace your roots, but don't let them limit you. You are not defined by one place, culture, or language. You are a mosaic, and every piece of your identity is valuable. You are the root; the branches will grow in ways you never imagined.

Closing Reflection

"In my childhood's shadows, I found my deepest scars and greatest strength. And now, I hope those lessons can guide you toward a brighter path."

Looking back, I realize my childhood was not just painful—it was instructive. The darkness that surrounded me taught me how to survive, adapt, and transform pain into power. But it also came with a cost. I became a survival expert, but I forgot how to live.

To my son: I share this not to burden you but to free you. I do not want you to carry the weight of my past—I want you to learn from it. Don't let the darkness define you as it once did me. Let it shape you, but never consume you. Life will test you, and there will be moments when you question who you are and where you belong. I hope you will never need to wear masks like I did. Be unapologetically yourself, even when the world tells you otherwise. You are not the product of my failures; you are the promise of something better.

Chapter 2:

Lessons from Failure

"Failure isn't the end. It's the crack in the foundation where the light of growth begins to seep through."

If there's one universal truth I've come to accept, failure is inevitable. It comes in many forms: missed opportunities, broken relationships, choices we can't undo, and the haunting mistakes we wish we could take back. But failure isn't just a momentary setback; it's a powerful mirror, showing us where we've faltered and, more importantly, where we can rise again. No matter how crushing, every failure is an opportunity to rebuild, reframe, and grow.

I've faced failure in every corner of my life: friendships that crumbled, family bonds strained to their breaking point, romantic connections that unraveled, and even within myself—when I became a stranger in my mind. Each failure left a mark, but those marks became the map of my growth. They weren't scars to be hidden; they were road signs pointing to the lessons I needed to learn.

Failure, I've learned, isn't the enemy we often make it out to be. It's the teacher we so often ignore. The greatest lessons are the ones that sting the most, that shake us at our core. But those lessons carry the most power, changing us for the better, even when we can't see it in the moment. The key is how we respond to failure, how we let it shape us—or how we let it break us.

The Cost of Betraying Myself

"Sometimes the greatest betrayal isn't from others—it's from yourself."

One of my earliest lessons in failure came from a moment I'll never forget. I was performing in a school magic show. Magic had always been my refuge—a craft that allowed me to create awe and manipulate reality in ways that made people believe in the impossible. It was my sanctuary, where I could escape the world's weight and transform into someone else.

But one day, everything went wrong. A trick failed, spectacularly and publicly. Instead of being stunned into silence, the audience erupted in laughter. Their laughter wasn't kind. It wasn't filled with humor—it was sharp, piercing, and unrelenting. It cut through my confidence like a blade, exposing a vulnerability I wasn't prepared to confront.

In that moment, I had a choice: to stand tall in my failure, to own it, or to hide in plain sight. I chose the latter. I joined in their laughter, pretending I was in on the joke. It felt like survival, like deflecting the blow before it could land. But deep down, I knew something had broken inside of me. I had betrayed myself, my passion, and my art.

That moment wasn't just about a failed trick—it was the first time I betrayed myself. Instead of embracing the vulnerability that failure offered, I transformed from a magician, a creator of awe, into a clown—someone who performed not to inspire but to amuse at their own expense. I chose to diminish myself to make others feel comfortable. I sacrificed my truth for the sake of fitting in.

Looking back, I see that laughing at myself wasn't resilience but avoidance. Instead of facing the failure head-on, I buried it beneath layers of humor. But with each laugh, I chipped away at my own identity. I disconnected from the essence of who I was, allowing the opinions of others to dictate my sense of self-worth.

To my son: When you fail—and you will—don't hide from it. Don't laugh it off to make others feel comfortable. Stand tall in your failure. Own it. Learn from it. And never diminish yourself for anyone. There is great strength in vulnerability. There's magic not in perfection but in the courage to continue performing, no matter how many times you stumble.

The Friendships That Fell Apart

"Not everyone who walks with you is meant to stay by your side."

Failure isn't always about what you do; sometimes, it's about what you fail to do. Over the years, I've lost friends—not because of betrayal or malice, but because I failed to be the person they needed me to be at that moment. I failed to show up in the ways they needed me, and in doing so, I lost the connection.

I once had a friend who confided in me during one of the hardest times in their lives. They didn't want advice or solutions; they simply wanted someone to listen. But I, in my usual way, was focused on being "helpful." I interrupted with suggestions, dismissed their emotions with logic, and tried to offer answers when all they needed was silence—my presence without an agenda.

Our friendship faded after that. At the time, I didn't understand why, but now I realize that sometimes, failure isn't loud or obvious. It's the quiet moments, the subtle neglect when we fail to show up for someone who needs us. It's the missed opportunities to simply be there—without judgment or fixing- just as a silent companion.

Another friendship fell apart because I let my insecurities poison it. I envied their confidence, success, and seemingly effortless ability to navigate life. Instead of being happy for them, I withdrew. I distanced myself, convincing myself it was because I no longer belonged in their world. The truth? I let my feelings of inadequacy push them away. I wasn't secure enough to share in their joy without making it about my own perceived shortcomings.

To my son: Relationships are fragile and require more than effort—they require understanding, empathy, and presence. Listen more than you speak. Be present not to solve problems but to support them. And when you fail, as I have, let it teach you to do better next time. Friendship is a gift, but it's also a responsibility. Treat it with care and gentleness, and you'll find that the bonds you build will withstand the test of time.

The Lies We Tell Ourselves

"The easiest person to lie to is yourself, and the hardest truth to face is your reflection."

One of my greatest failures was losing myself in the lies I told to survive. We all tell ourselves stories about who we are, what we need, and how we're supposed to behave. But the deeper I sank into these stories, the more disconnected I became from the truth. I told myself that my success defined me, that I was invincible, and that the personas I created were who I truly was. But as I told myself these lies, I began to lose touch with the reality of who I was becoming.

I told myself I didn't care about the teasing, that I didn't need real friends, and that my ability to manipulate situations to my advantage was a strength. But these lies were not shields—they were chains. They kept me from confronting the truth: that I was lonely, that I was scared, and that I had no idea who I was anymore.

One day, the weight of these lies became too much to bear. It wasn't a dramatic breakdown but a quiet, almost imperceptible shift. I looked in the mirror and didn't recognize the person staring back. The achievements I had worked so hard for felt hollow. The personas I had created to protect myself had become prisons. They kept me safe, yes, but they also kept me from truly living.

To my son: Don't lose yourself in the lies you tell yourself to get through the day. They may seem comforting, but they will only distance you from your identity. Face your fears, your failures, and your flaws with honesty. The truth may be painful, but it will also set you free. Embrace who you are, even when it's messy, even when it's imperfect. Authenticity is the only path to true peace.

Failing at Love

"Love teaches us the most, not in its presence, but in its loss."

Romantic failure carries its unique sting. It bruises your ego—it shakes your very foundation. Over the years, I've experienced relationships falling apart, not because I didn't care but because I cared incorrectly.

I thought love was about providing and showing strength and capability. I thought being a good partner meant being invulnerable, always in control, always "fixing" the problems that arose. But love isn't a transaction—it's a connection. And connection requires vulnerability.

One of the hardest lessons I learned was that walls, no matter how high or well-built, don't protect love. They isolate it. I failed to let my partners see my fears, insecurities, and doubts; in doing so, I denied them the chance to truly know me. Love can't thrive behind a fortress; it needs openness. It needs trust. And I, in my misguided need to control, kept love at arm's length.

To my son: When you love, love fully. Let your guard down. Be strong enough to be vulnerable. Love isn't about perfection—it's about connection. And when love fails, don't let it harden your heart. Let it teach you, and let each loss bring you closer to the kind of love you deserve.

Failures in Courage

"Sometimes, failing to act is the greatest failure of all."

There were moments in my life when I stood at a crossroads, knowing exactly what I should do but being too afraid to take that leap. Whether speaking up for myself, standing up for someone else, or seizing an opportunity, I let fear paralyze me. Fear of rejection, failure, and the unknown— all of these fears robbed me of precious moments I'll never get back.

And inaction, I've learned, is a choice. It's a silent failure that carries its kind of regret that you can't shake because it's rooted in the missed chances to make a difference.

To my son: Courage isn't the absence of fear; it's moving forward despite it. Don't let fear be the reason you stand still. Even when the path is uncertain, take that first step. There's more strength in trying and failing than never trying. Let courage be your guide, and the rest will follow.

The Missteps in Leadership

"A true leader learns from their mistakes."

In my career and personal life, I've often been put in positions where others looked to me for guidance. I wanted to lead well and inspire confidence and trust. But leadership isn't about being perfect—it's about being human.

Sometimes, I made decisions out of pride, refusing to admit when I didn't have all the answers. There were other times when I hesitated to make decisions, afraid of making the wrong choice. Both missteps taught me the same lesson: leadership isn't about always getting it right; it's about owning and learning from your mistakes.

To my son: When you lead, lead with humility. Admit when you're wrong, listen to those you guide, and never let pride stop you from growing. Leadership is a journey, not a destination.

The Beauty of Falling

"Why do we fall? So we can learn to pick ourselves up."

— Batman Begins

Failure is not the enemy. It's the harshest, most honest teacher you'll ever have. Every failure has taught me something invaluable—not just about the world but about myself.

I've learned that failure isn't the end; it's the beginning of growth. It's the moment when you decide whether to stay down or rise again. And with every rise, you become stronger, wiser, and more resilient.

To my son: Don't fear failure. Embrace it. Learn from it. Let it be the fire that forges your strength, not the weight that holds you down. With each fall, you learn how to rise higher.

Closing Reflection

"Failure doesn't define you. What you do next does."

Reflecting on my failures, I see them not as regrets but as stepping stones. Each one taught me a lesson I might never have learned otherwise. And now, I hope those lessons will help you navigate your journey.

To my son: Fall, rise, and keep moving forward. The path isn't always easy, but it's worth walking. Every misstep brings you closer to your true self.

Chapter 3:

The Price of Success

The Price of Success

"Success is a polished mirror that reflects only what others see—but behind it lies the cracks no one notices."

From the outside, success is dazzling. It's the applause, the recognition, and the envy of those around you. It looks like the ultimate achievement—the prize you work toward your entire life. But beneath the surface, success can take a heavy toll. It's not just about what you gain but what you lose in the pursuit.

For me, success was both a blessing and a curse. I was born with a sharp mind and quick hands, talents that made learning effortless and achieving easy. I could pick up skills faster than most, diving headfirst into anything interesting. But talent is a double-edged sword. It can elevate you but also isolate you, blind you, and trap you in expectations you didn't ask for.

The Weight of Talent

"When everything comes easily, you stop appreciating the value of effort."

As a child, I excelled at almost everything I tried. Sports, academics, hobbies—I thrived in all of them. I was on multiple school teams: track and field, swimming, basketball, and handball. I joined clubs, from chess to art to magic, and I didn't just participate—I stood out. But standing out came at a price.

I thought my accomplishments would make me popular and that success would win me friendships. But instead, it won me envy. My classmates didn't see me as someone to admire—they saw me as someone to exploit. They copied my homework, relied on me during group projects, and cheered for me only to watch me stumble. I was a pawn in their games, a tool to be used, and my achievements made them feel small, which made them want to see me fail.

One performance mistake during a school event was all it took. The same people who had praised me were now laughing at me, their mockery louder than any applause I'd ever received. I stood there, humiliated and exposed, feeling as though all of my previous accomplishments had amounted to nothing. The weight of the spotlight was no longer a symbol of pride—it became a constant pressure to maintain an impossible standard.

To cope, I laughed with them. I betrayed myself, turning my pain into their entertainment. It was the first time I realized that success when misused, can strip you of your humanity.

Instead of learning from my failure, I let their laughter consume it. My natural response to pain was to hide it behind a smile, but in doing so, I lost a piece of myself.

To my son: Your talents are gifts, but don't let them define you. Remember that they come with responsibility—not to others, but to yourself. Don't use them to chase validation from people who don't matter. Success is fleeting, but who you are, underneath it all, is what will last. Protect that.

The Illusion of Effortlessness

"When you succeed too easily, you stop asking why you're succeeding."

The ease with which I excelled wasn't always an advantage. It made me complacent, lazy in my thinking, and sloppy in my decisions. I relied so heavily on my natural abilities that I never learned to truly challenge myself. The results came too easily, and that's where the danger lay.

I began to take success for granted. Because it came so effortlessly, I didn't appreciate the hard work or the thought that went into it. I didn't seek out knowledge beyond what was immediately necessary. I didn't see the value in struggle or failure. I thought my abilities would carry me through life without much effort, and in doing so, I missed out on the deeper learning that comes with overcoming adversity.

This weakness became most apparent when I started working with others. I expected everyone to operate as efficiently as I did, understand things quickly, and perform without hesitation. But life doesn't work that way. People don't all move at the same pace, and when you rely too much on yourself, you alienate the people you need. I remember a group project where I took on most of the work because I didn't trust my teammates to keep up. At first, I felt like I was saving the project. But when it came time to present, I realized I'd deprived the group of their chance to contribute, and I'd overburdened myself in the process.

In my desire for control, I learned too late that true collaboration isn't about doing everything yourself; it's about trusting others to contribute and bring their talents to the table. By not allowing others to rise to the occasion, I limited the project and, more importantly, my growth.

To my son: Don't let your talents become a crutch. Use them to support others, not to overshadow them. Understand that success is never about standing alone—it's about building something together. Your gifts should inspire others, not isolate them. Collaboration is about building together, not carrying the weight alone.

The Sacrifices We Don't See

"For every success, something must be left behind."

Success demands sacrifices—time, energy, relationships, even parts of yourself. But what I didn't realize at the time was how much I was giving up for the sake of achievement. I was so focused on climbing the ladder that I failed to notice what was being left behind in the shadows.

I sacrificed friendships, choosing work over connection. I sacrificed self-care, pushing myself beyond my limits to chase perfection. I sacrificed authenticity, becoming what I thought others wanted me to be. I buried parts of myself so deep that I forgot they were there.

It wasn't until much later that I understood the cost. Success without balance leaves you empty. It's a house built on a hollow foundation—beautiful on the outside but crumbling within. Achieving all my goals didn't bring me peace; it brought me exhaustion, loneliness, and a sense that something crucial was missing. The victories felt hollow. I'd spent so much time chasing the next prize that I hadn't invested in the people or practices that would have truly nourished me.

To my son: Don't sacrifice who you are for what you achieve. Success is meaningless if it leaves you hollow. Chase it, but not at the expense of your relationships, health, or identity. The truest form of success is one that leaves you whole—not one that leaves you broken. Make time for what matters, for the people who love you, and for the things that give your life.

The Pressure of Expectations

"When others expect you to succeed, failure feels twice as heavy."

Success brings attention, and with attention comes expectation. The more I achieved, the more people expected from me. Teachers, friends, even family—they saw my potential and projected their hopes onto me. At first, I thrived under the pressure, believing I could live up to it. But over time, the weight of their expectations became suffocating.

I stopped pursuing things because I enjoyed them. Instead, I pursued them to meet the standards others had set for me. Every success felt less like a victory and more like a fleeting moment of relief before the next challenge. I wasn't living for myself—I was performing for others. The applause that once felt fulfilling now became a burden. The expectations grew higher, and the room for error became smaller. With each success, the fear of failure intensified.

To my son: Success is a gift, but don't let it become a burden. Set your own goals and measure your worth by your own standards. It's your life to live, not theirs. The weight of others' expectations can feel like an anchor, but your true worth lies in following your own path, not in trying to satisfy everyone else. Seek your own meaning, and you'll find peace.

The Shadows of Comparison

"The moment you compare your success to others, you begin to lose sight of your own worth."

No matter how much I achieved, it never felt like enough. I looked around and saw others who seemed to have more—more talent, more recognition, more fulfillment. Comparison turned my accomplishments and disappointments, my milestones into reminders of how far I still had to go. It created a constant cycle of insecurity, where no matter what I achieved, someone else's success always loomed larger.

This habit of comparing didn't just steal my joy—it fueled my insecurities. It made me question my abilities and doubt my worth. I was running a race against people who didn't even know they were competing with me. It wasn't about the joy of succeeding—it was about staying ahead of everyone else, about making sure I wasn't left behind.

To my son: Success is personal. Don't measure it against others because their journey isn't yours. Celebrate their victories, but never let them diminish your own. The only race you need to run is the one against yourself. Strive to be better than you were yesterday, and you'll find fulfillment in your own growth. Comparison only steals your peace.

When Success Is a Mask

"Sometimes, we use success to hide from the things we don't want to face."

There were times when I used success as a distraction, a way to avoid dealing with deeper issues. If I was excelling, no one would question how I was feeling. If I was achieving, no one would see the cracks forming beneath the surface. Success became my armor, a way to deflect attention from my own fears and insecurities.

But hiding behind success only works for so long. Eventually, the mask slips, and you're forced to confront the very things you were running from. For me, it was loneliness, self-doubt, and the fear that my success wasn't enough to make me truly happy. I had convinced myself that I could outrun my problems by being successful, but I learned that success can't protect you from your inner demons.

To my son: Success can be a mask, but it shouldn't be. Face your struggles head-on, even when it's uncomfortable. True strength comes from acknowledging your vulnerabilities, not hiding them. Don't use success to cover up your pain. The most important thing you can do is learn to embrace who you are, flaws and all.

Redefining Success

"True success isn't about what you gain—it's about who you become."

For years, I have let others define success for me. It was grades, trophies, titles, applause. But none of those things brought me the fulfillment I thought they would. They were empty markers of achievement that never satisfied my deeper need for meaning.

It wasn't until I began to question what success meant to me that I found clarity. Success isn't external—it's internal. It's living a life that aligns with your values, pursuing what truly matters to you, and finding joy in the process, not just the outcome. It's about growth, relationships, and becoming the person, you're meant to be—not chasing a prize or an image.

To my son: Define success on your own terms. Don't chase it for others; chase it for yourself. If success means peace, pursue it. If it means growth, fight for it. But make sure it's yours. Don't let the world tell you what success looks like—create your own definition and follow it with all your heart.

Closing Reflection

"Success without purpose is a gilded cage. Success with meaning is freedom."

As I reflect on the successes I've had and the price I paid for them, I see them not as regrets but as lessons. They taught me what truly matters, what's worth sacrificing for, and what isn't. Success is beautiful when it's aligned with purpose, but it's hollow if it's chased without intention. The greatest success isn't in what you achieve but in how you live.

To my son: Your talents are gifts, but your choices define your legacy. Use your gifts wisely, pursue success thoughtfully, and never forget that the greatest success is living a life that feels true to you. Follow your own path, and let that be your success.

THE CORE

LESSONS

Chapter 4:

The Power of Resilience

The Power of Resilience

"Resilience is not about how many times life knocks you down—it's about finding the courage to rise, no matter how heavy the burden."

If life is a battlefield, resilience is your armor. It doesn't promise you'll avoid pain or hardship, but it ensures you'll endure it. Resilience isn't a trait you're born with—it's something you build, piece by piece, through every challenge you face.

For me, resilience wasn't just a lesson—it was a necessity. Every fall, every failure, every moment of darkness demanded it. And though the journey wasn't easy, it was resilience that gave me the strength to move forward, no matter the cost. Without it, I would have stayed buried in my own despair. But with resilience, I learned to rise. Over and over again.

The Roots of Resilience

"We fall not to stay down but to discover the strength it takes to rise again."

My earliest lessons in resilience were born out of necessity. As a child, I grew up surrounded by the chaos of a fractured home. There was constant noise—arguments, confusion, and a sense that nothing would ever be steady or certain. My world seemed like it was always on the edge of falling apart. And in that environment, I had two choices: succumb to the weight of my circumstances or find a way to stand tall in spite of them.

I remember one night, after a particularly harsh argument at home. I sat alone in my room, the silence pressing down on me, almost suffocating. My instinct was to let the sadness consume me, to crawl into that space of pain and despair where I could hide from everything. But something inside me pushed back against it. I grabbed a notebook and began to write. I wrote down everything I wanted to become: strong, independent, unshakable. These were not just words to me—they were a declaration.

That list became my guidepost. A constant reminder that no matter how heavy the world became, I could always choose my response. Whenever life tried to break me, I looked back at it. I reminded myself I can't control what happens to me, but I can control what I do next. And what I chose to do was rise.

Resilience started with that choice. It was a decision to keep moving forward, even when the path was unclear, even when I didn't know how I'd make it through. That first step was the hardest, but it was also the most important. Every time I rose, I grew stronger—even if it didn't feel like it at the moment.

To my son: Resilience starts with a choice. Life will challenge you in ways you can't predict, but you always have the power to decide how you respond. The first step is always the hardest, but it's also the one that sets the course for everything that comes next. Every time you rise, you'll grow stronger, even if it doesn't feel like it at the moment. Keep going, no matter what.

Mental Resilience—The Fortress of the Mind

"Your mind is your strongest ally, but only if you train it to be."

The world is loud. Doubts, fears, and insecurities bombard you daily, and the strongest attacks often come from within. The thoughts in your head can either empower you or paralyze you. Mental resilience is the art of quieting that noise, of discerning what truly matters, and of focusing on the possibilities rather than the limitations.

When I was younger, self-doubt was my constant companion. I would start projects with enthusiasm, but the minute things didn't go as planned, I would abandon them. The weight of my own insecurities felt too heavy to bear. I questioned my abilities, second-guessed my choices, and allowed fear to control me.

But there came a turning point when I realized that my thoughts weren't facts—they were just voices, and I had the power to decide which ones to listen to. This was the first lesson in mental resilience: not every thought deserves your attention. The voices that tell you "you're not good enough" or "you can't do this" are not the truth—they're simply noise.

I started practicing what I now call "mental triage." Whenever my mind was overwhelmed, I would stop and ask myself: What's real? What can I control? I focused on the facts, the present moment, and the things I had the power to change. This simple act of sorting my thoughts gave me clarity and helped me push forward, even when fear threatened to hold me back.

As time went on, I learned the importance of self-talk. Instead of criticizing myself, I began speaking to myself with the same kindness and encouragement I would offer to a friend. Instead of thinking, *"I'm not good enough,"* I thought, *"I am capable, and I will keep moving forward."* Slowly, my mind became a place of refuge instead of a battlefield.

To my son: Your mind is your most powerful ally, but you must train it to serve you. Not every thought is worth your attention. Let in the thoughts that serve you and shut out the ones that don't. Clarity is your greatest weapon and kindness toward yourself is your greatest strength. Be patient with your mind, and it will become your fortress.

Emotional Resilience—Carrying the Weight of the Heart

"A resilient heart isn't one that avoids pain—it's one that transforms it."

Emotional resilience isn't about suppressing your feelings—it's about understanding them, processing them, and transforming them into fuel for growth. I learned this lesson the hard way.

I remember a time when heartbreak left me shattered. I had poured so much of myself into a relationship, believing that it would fill the voids I felt inside. I had put all my hope into someone else, thinking they could somehow fix the emptiness I felt within. But when that relationship ended, it felt like losing a part of my very identity. For weeks, I couldn't see a way forward. I avoided the places we had been, the music we had listened to, and even the friends we had shared. Everything became too painful to bear.

But in the midst of that pain, I had a revelation: Pain is temporary, but the strength it leaves behind is permanent. I allowed myself to grieve, to feel the depth of my sadness. But I also reminded myself that I would heal. It wasn't easy, and it wasn't quick, but I made a choice not to let my grief define me. Instead, I used it as a reminder of my capacity to feel deeply—and my ability to heal.

Over time, I realized that emotional resilience is not about avoiding pain or pretending it doesn't exist. It's about honoring your feelings, allowing them to pass through you, and finding the lessons they have to offer. Every heartbreak every disappointment, left me stronger, wiser, and more capable of facing the future with an open heart.

To my son: Your heart will break, but it will also rebuild. Don't be afraid of your emotions—let yourself feel, but never let those feelings control you. Strength comes from the courage to heal, even when it feels impossible. Pain is a part of life, but it doesn't last forever. What remains is your ability to grow and love again. Trust in your resilience.

Resilience Through Community

"Even the strongest among us need someone to lean on."

Resilience isn't a solo act. While much of it comes from within, the people around you play a crucial role. I've learned that leaning on others doesn't make you weak—it makes you human. We all have moments when we need help, and that's okay.

For much of my life, I tried to shoulder everything alone. I believed that asking for help was a sign of failure and that if I was truly strong, I could do it all on my own. But during one of the lowest points in my life, a friend reached out to me. They didn't wait for me to ask—they simply offered their support, their presence, and their kindness. It was exactly what I needed, even though I hadn't known it at the time.

That moment changed my perspective. I realized that resilience doesn't mean isolation—it means knowing when to accept the strength of others. At that moment, I understood that community is essential to resilience. Friends, mentors, and even strangers who show kindness—all of these people became pillars that supported me when I couldn't stand on my own.

Resilience is not just about your own strength—it's about the strength you draw from those around you. Building a community of people who believe in you, who challenge you, and who will stand by you when the world feels heavy is one of the most important things you can do.

To my son: Build your community. Surround yourself with people who lift you up, who challenge you, and who remind you that you are not alone. Resilience is strongest when shared. There is no shame in asking for help—it's a sign of wisdom, not weakness. When you allow others to support you, you allow them to be a part of your journey.

Resilience in Failure—Rising from the Ashes

"Failure is the greatest teacher, but only if you're willing to learn."

Every failure I've faced has taught me something valuable, even if I didn't see it at the time. The key is to look at failure not as an ending but as a beginning—a chance to start over, stronger and wiser.

I once failed spectacularly at a project into which I had poured months of hard work. The disappointment was crushing, and for days, I questioned me

abilities and whether I was capable of succeeding at all. But after the initial shock and grief, I did something important: I stopped wallowing. I started analyzing, breaking down what went wrong and what I could do better next time. I discovered that failure doesn't just test your resilience—it builds it.

Each time you rise from failure, you prove to yourself that you are stronger than the obstacles in your path. Failure isn't something to fear; it's a valuable tool for growth. The lessons it teaches are worth every moment of discomfort because those lessons make you better.

To my son: Don't fear failure. Embrace it. Every time you fail, take a moment to learn from it. The lessons you gain are more valuable than success without struggle. Every failure is a stepping stone on the path to greatness.

Spiritual Resilience—Finding Light in the Darkness

"In the darkest moments, it's often faith—in yourself, in others, in something greater—that keeps you going."

Spiritual resilience is about finding strength in something bigger than yourself. It's about the belief that even in the most challenging times, there's a reason to keep going. For me, spiritual resilience wasn't about religion—it was about the quiet faith that no matter how hard things became, there would always be something worth fighting for.

During my lowest points, I found solace in small moments of beauty: the warmth of sunlight on my face, the sound of laughter, and the quiet peace of a late-night sky. These simple things reminded me that even in the darkest times, there's light if you're willing to look for it.

To my son: Find your light, and let it guide you when the world feels overwhelming. It doesn't have to be grand or dramatic—it just has to remind you that life is worth fighting for. Whether it's love, hope, or the beauty of a single moment, let it be your anchor in the storm.

The Beauty of Scars

"Scars aren't flaws—they're evidence of your journey."

Every scar, every mark left by life's challenges, tells a story. They don't define you, but they are a part of you—a testament to your resilience. Over time, I've come to see my scars not as reminders of pain but as symbols of survival.

Some scars are visible, etched into the skin by the hardships of life. Others are invisible, etched into the soul. But all scars carry the same message: You survived. You endured. You grew stronger.

To my son: Wear your scars proudly. They are proof that you faced life's battles and emerged stronger. They are a reminder that even in the face of adversity, you choose to keep going.

Closing Reflection

"Resilience isn't just the ability to rise—it's the courage to keep rising, no matter how many times you fall."

To my son: Life will challenge you in ways you can't predict. But know this: you have the strength to overcome anything it throws your way. Nurture your mind, guard your heart, and find your light in the darkest moments. Resilience will be your greatest ally, and it will carry you further than you ever thought possible. Keep rising, and never stop.

Chapter 5:

The Balance of Strength and Empathy

The Balance of Strength and Empathy

"Strength without empathy is a sword without a hilt—powerful but dangerous to wield. True greatness lies in balancing power with understanding."

For much of my life, I believed that strength meant control. Control over circumstances, over emotions, over people. I saw empathy as a distraction—something that made you vulnerable, a weakness that could be exploited. I was driven by ambition, and I believed that to succeed, I needed to be tough and to push through challenges without giving in to emotions. The more I leaned into strength, the more I distanced myself from others. But time, as it often does, taught me that this approach had its limits.

One of the hardest lessons I learned was this: strength without empathy isn't strength at all—it's isolation. Real strength isn't about dominating or controlling; it's about holding space for others, understanding their struggles, and connecting with them on a human level. Strength without empathy can protect you, but it can also isolate you. Empathy without strength, on the other hand, leaves you vulnerable to being overwhelmed by the needs of others. True greatness lies in finding the balance between the two—strength tempered with understanding.

The older I got, the more I realized that to be truly strong, I had to be willing to see the world through the eyes of others. That means not just hearing their words but feeling their emotions, recognizing their struggles, and allowing their experiences to shape my responses. This balance doesn't come easily, especially for those of us who are driven by ambition and fueled by the desire to overcome, but it's a balance worth striving for.

The Sword and the Shield

"Strength protects; empathy connects. Both are essential in a world that demands resilience and understanding."

Strength and empathy are often seen as opposites, but in truth, they complement each other. Strength is the sword that defends you from harm, while empathy is the shield that softens the blows you deliver to others. One without the other is incomplete.

I learned this lesson the hard way. There was a time when I wielded my strength carelessly, thinking that being strong meant always winning. I remember a heated argument with a close friend where my focus was on winning rather than understanding. I used my words as weapons, cutting deep to prove my point. I was right, but at what cost? Though I won the argument, I lost something far more valuable—the trust and connection we had built.

It took years to repair that relationship and even longer to realize the truth: strength isn't about dominating others—it's about protecting what matters without destroying it in the process. Strength should protect, not harm. It should be used to defend those you love and care for and to uphold what you believe in without trampling over others in the process.

Empathy, on the other hand, is the shield that protects relationships. It softens the impact of our actions, even when we need to be firm. Without empathy, even the most righteous cause can leave destruction in its wake. But with empathy, strength becomes something that uplifts instead of tears down.

To my son: Be strong, but be kind. Let your strength protect, not harm. And let your empathy guide the way. The balance of these two will allow you to navigate life's challenges without leaving destruction in your wake. True power comes when both are in harmony.

Empathy as a Leadership Tool

"A leader who lacks empathy commands fear; a leader who possesses it inspires loyalty."

Empathy isn't just a virtue—it's a skill and one of the most powerful tools in leadership. Whether you're leading a team, a family, or simply managing your own life, the ability to understand others is what sets true leaders apart. Leadership isn't just about making decisions—it's about making decisions that take the well-being of others into account.

I remember working on a team where the leader was brilliant but cold. Their intelligence was unmatched, but their inability to connect with the team bred resentment. People didn't feel seen. They didn't feel heard. Tasks were completed out of obligation, not inspiration, and the atmosphere was heavy with tension. No matter how many hours we worked, we weren't motivated by the leader's vision—we were motivated by the need to avoid confrontation.

Years later, I found myself in a similar leadership role. I remembered that experience and vowed to approach it differently. Instead of just focusing on the task at hand, I took time to understand the people I worked with. I made an effort to understand their fears, their motivations, and their struggles. I listened, really listened, to their ideas and concerns. The result was transformative: instead of working for me, they worked with me. We were a team united by mutual respect and understanding. And together, we achieved more than I ever could have alone.

Empathy doesn't just make you a better leader—it makes you a better person. When people know you understand them, they feel valued. And when people feel valued, they will move mountains for you. It's the foundation of trust. And trust is what inspires loyalty.

To my son: Lead with empathy. People will follow you not because they fear you but because they trust you. And that trust is worth more than any title or accolade you might earn. True leadership is about connection, not control. When you lead with empathy, you inspire others to rise with you.

The Cost of Imbalance

"Too much strength hardens the heart; too much empathy weakens the resolve. Balance is the key to harmony."

For a long time, I lived on one extreme. I was task-oriented, goal-driven, and focused on results above all else. I believed that showing vulnerability or prioritizing others' feelings was a waste of time. Emotions, I thought, were distractions. I couldn't afford to be weak. I had a goal, and I was determined to achieve it—no matter the cost.

But this mindset came at a significant price. I strained relationships with friends and family, pushing them away with my unrelenting focus on achievement. I missed countless moments of connection, blind to the needs of those around me. I was so consumed by my ambition that I failed to nurture the bonds that truly mattered.

Eventually, the loneliness became impossible to ignore. Despite my successes, I felt empty. I had sacrificed too much for the sake of productivity, and the results were evident. It was then that I began to understand that strength without empathy isolates you. It creates walls around you that prevent others from connecting. But empathy without strength leaves you vulnerable to being overwhelmed by the weight of others' needs. It creates a situation where you care so much for others that you forget to care for yourself.

Only by finding balance can you truly thrive. Strength allows you to pursue your goals with determination, while empathy keeps you connected to those around you. The key to harmony lies in balancing both, understanding when to push forward and when to hold back, when to be firm, and when to soften.

To my son: Don't let strength blind you, and don't let empathy weaken you. Strive for balance in all things. Life isn't about choosing one over the other—it's about integrating both into who you are. That's where true peace lies. You'll find that by striking this balance, you'll live a life that is both successful and fulfilling.

The Power of Vulnerability

"To be vulnerable is to show strength in its most human form."

For years, I saw vulnerability as a weakness. I thought opening up would make me a target and that showing emotion would undermine my authority. I believed that strength meant closing off, holding everything in, and appearing invulnerable to the world. But the truth is, vulnerability is one of the greatest strengths you can possess. It is the courage to show the world your human side—the side that feels pain, fear, joy, and hope.

I remember a time when I was struggling deeply but refused to admit it. I wore my strength like armor, but inside, I was crumbling. I feared that if people saw how broken I felt, they would lose faith in me. But in my attempt to protect myself, I alienated the very people who could help. It wasn't until I finally shared my struggles with someone, I trusted that I began to heal. That moment taught me that vulnerability doesn't diminish you—it connects you to others in a way nothing else can.

Opening up doesn't make you weak—it makes you real. And when you allow others to see your real self, they will offer you the same compassion and strength in return.

To my son: Don't be afraid to let others see your struggles. True strength isn't about hiding your pain—it's about facing it with courage and letting others help you through it. Vulnerability isn't a weakness; it's a strength that builds trust and deepens connections. Embrace it, and you'll find the support you need to grow.

Strength and Empathy in Action

"Strength without action is potentially wasted; empathy without action is care unfulfilled."

Balancing strength and empathy isn't just about intentions—it's about actions. It's about choosing to stand firm when it's easier to fold and choosing to show compassion when it's easier to ignore. The real test of this balance comes in moments of conflict when emotions run high and the temptation to react without thinking is strong.

It's in those moments where you must listen instead of retaliate, where you must protect without overpowering. I've learned that these moments define who you are—not just to others but to yourself. It's easy to be strong when everything is going your way, but it's in the tough moments that you truly demonstrate what kind of person you are.

To my son: Let your actions reflect the balance you seek. Be the person who others trust to be both strong and kind, firm and fair. It's not enough to just feel empathy or to be strong—you must show it in your actions. In doing so, you'll create a life that is both meaningful and impactful.

Empathy for Yourself

"You cannot truly understand others until you first understand yourself."

One of the hardest lessons I learned was that empathy must start inward. For years, I was my harshest critic. I held myself to impossible standards, demanding perfection from myself while offering compassion to others. When I inevitably fell short, I tore myself down. I wasn't just striving for success—I was striving for an unattainable ideal, and I punished myself when I couldn't reach it.

It wasn't until I began to practice self-compassion that I truly understood empathy. By acknowledging my own struggles and allowing myself to grow from them, I became better equipped to understand and support others. Self-compassion isn't about excusing your mistakes; it's about acknowledging them and giving yourself permission to learn and grow.

To my son: Be kind to yourself. You are human, and humans are imperfect. Extend to yourself the same empathy you would offer a friend, and you'll find that understanding others becomes much easier. When you treat yourself with compassion, you'll be better able to treat others the same way.

The Ripple Effect of Balance

"When you balance strength and empathy, you don't just change yourself—you change the world around you."

Strength and empathy are not just personal virtues—they are catalysts for change. When you embody this balance, you inspire others to do the same. Your actions create a ripple effect that shapes the relationships, communities, and systems you're a part of.

I've seen this firsthand in my own life. When I began to lead with empathy, it transformed my relationships. When I chose to stand firm with kindness, it encouraged others to do the same. This balance doesn't just benefit you—it benefits everyone you touch. By modeling strength and empathy, you encourage others to be their best selves, too.

To my son: Remember that your strength and empathy have the power to impact more than just your own life. Use them wisely, and you'll leave a legacy that extends far beyond yourself. Your actions, no matter how small, have the power to ripple outward and change the world. Choose wisely.

Closing Reflection

"The strongest people aren't those who stand alone—they're the ones who lift others up while carrying their own burdens with grace."

To my son: Strength and empathy are not opposites—they are partners. Use your strength to protect and your empathy to connect. Together, they will guide you through life's challenges and help you build a legacy that lasts. Be both strong and kind, firm and fair. And remember, the true test of greatness isn't how much you achieve—it's how you make others feel along the way.

Chapter 6:

The Art of Thinking

Clearly

The Art of Thinking Clearly

"A clear mind is not one free of doubt, but one that sees doubt for what it is: a shadow, not a wall."

Clarity of thought is often misunderstood as the absence of doubt or confusion. However, true mental clarity isn't about eliminating uncertainty—it's about recognizing and managing it. A clear mind is not one that is free of doubt but one that understands doubt as a natural part of the process, something to be acknowledged, not feared. The ability to see doubt for what it is—just a shadow—gives you the power to move forward with intention and purpose.

For much of my life, I believed that intelligence alone would be enough to succeed. I was convinced that cleverness and quick thinking were all I needed to overcome obstacles and make good decisions. But over time, I learned the hard way that clarity of thought is far more valuable than raw intellect. It's the difference between reacting impulsively and responding thoughtfully, between rushing into situations and moving with purpose.

True mental clarity is the compass that keeps you on course in the chaotic seas of life. Without it, you're like a ship adrift, tossed by the waves of emotion and circumstance. But when you cultivate clarity, you become the captain of your destiny, able to navigate challenges with precision, even when the path forward is unclear.

The Discipline of Mental Clarity

"A cluttered mind makes cluttered choices. Clear your thoughts, and your path will reveal itself."

The mind is like a garden. If you don't tend to it, weeds of doubt, fear, and distraction will overtake it. But if you nurture it with care, it can become a source of strength and clarity, even in the most challenging times.

For years, I lived with a mind that was anything but clear. I was juggling too many responsibilities, trying to meet the expectations of others, and constantly feeling like I was falling behind. Each decision I made seemed to carry the weight of uncertainty. I was overwhelmed, and the noise in my head only grew louder the harder I tried to quiet it. The constant rush to respond to every demand and the fear of making mistakes—all led to a vicious cycle of stress and poor decision-making.

It wasn't until I learned the discipline of "mental stillness" that I found peace. I began setting aside regular time to reflect, to clear my mind, and to sort through my thoughts. I treated my mind like a messy desk: I took the time to sort through the papers—what was urgent? What was important? What could wait? By creating this space for reflection, I found that the more I cleared my thoughts, the more clearly I could see my path forward.

Mental stillness isn't about avoiding thoughts but rather organizing them in a way that allows you to make decisions with confidence and intention. This practice became my anchor, helping me stay grounded in the face of uncertainty.

To my son: Guard your mind. It is the most powerful tool you have. Don't let it be overwhelmed by distractions or negativity. Clear your thoughts regularly, and you will find the strength to face any challenge with clarity and purpose.

The Power of Strategic Thinking

"In a world full of moves, the one who thinks ahead controls the board."

Life is like a complex game of chess, and strategy is your greatest asset. It's not enough to react to the moves of others; you must anticipate their next steps, plan your own moves carefully, and think several steps ahead. Life is not about being the fastest or the most reactive; it's about being the most strategic.

I remember a particular period in my career when I was competing for a promotion. My colleague was, on paper, far more qualified than I was. The position was theirs to lose. But rather than focusing on my colleague's strengths, I focused on my own. I analyzed the role, recognized where my unique skills could offer value, and devised a plan to highlight how I could contribute in ways my colleagues couldn't. I didn't just focus on the end goal; I thought through the process and anticipated what would set me apart. I made a conscious effort to show how my abilities and perspective were critical to the team's success.

When the promotion came my way, it wasn't because I was the smartest or the most experienced—it was because I had a strategy. I thought ahead, played to my strengths, and made my moves with intention.

To my son: Never rush into decisions without a plan. Take the time to think through your options, anticipate challenges, and develop a strategy. Life is full of obstacles, but if you can approach each challenge with a clear plan, you will not only overcome them but also turn them into opportunities.

Understanding Others—The Key to Clarity

"The clearest path is often hidden in the hearts and minds of those around you."

Clear thinking isn't just about understanding yourself—it's about understanding others. People are often the most unpredictable variables in any situation, and the ability to read them, to see beyond their words and actions, is an invaluable skill. People rarely behave the way we expect, and misjudging their intentions can lead to confusion and misdirection. True clarity comes from understanding others, from seeing situations from their perspective, and from recognizing that the choices of those around you often shape your own path.

I remember a time when I misjudged someone terribly. I assumed they were acting out of selfishness and that their actions were calculated and malicious. I treated them with distrust, keeping my distance. But when I finally took the time to listen—to truly hear them and understand their perspective—I realized I had been wrong. Their actions weren't driven by malice; they were struggling in ways I hadn't seen, facing challenges of their own. My assumptions had clouded my judgment, and my relationship with them suffered because of it.

That experience taught me that when you approach others with curiosity rather than judgment, you gain clarity. People are rarely what they seem at first glance, and the more you understand their struggles, their fears, and their motivations, the clearer your perspective becomes. By fostering empathy and seeking understanding, you create the conditions for clarity in your relationships and decisions.

To my son: Seek to understand before you judge. People are often much more complex than they appear at first glance, and the more you understand them, the clearer your own path will be. Remember, clarity often comes from listening, not speaking.

Decision-Making in the Face of Uncertainty

"Not every choice will be clear, but every choice will teach you something."

One of the hardest truths I've learned in life is that you'll often have to make decisions without all the information you need. Clarity doesn't mean having all the answers; it means having the courage to act, even when the outcome is uncertain. The process of making a decision in the face of uncertainty requires confidence, self-awareness, and an understanding that even if the decision turns out wrong, it's still an opportunity to learn.

I've made countless decisions that felt like leaps of faith. Some worked out, some didn't. But in each case, I gained something valuable—a lesson, an insight, a new perspective.

The key isn't to avoid mistakes but to make decisions based on your core values, not your fears. When you align your choices with what truly matters to you, even failure becomes an important step forward. Mistakes are just stepping stones on the way to wisdom.

To my son: Don't let fear paralyze you. Trust your instincts, act with intention, and remember that clarity doesn't come from avoiding mistakes—it comes from learning from them. Every decision, no matter the outcome, is an opportunity to grow.

The Art of Letting Go

"Clarity isn't just about knowing what to hold onto—it's about knowing what to release."

Sometimes, the greatest obstacle to clear thinking is holding onto things that no longer serve you. Whether it's a failed dream, a toxic relationship, or an outdated belief, the weight of these things can cloud your judgment and keep you from moving forward.

I once held onto a project for far too long, even though it was clear that it wasn't going to succeed. I was so attached to the idea of finishing what I'd started that I ignored all the signs telling me to let go. I refused to admit that it was time to move on. But when I finally walked away from the project, I felt a weight lift off my shoulders. Suddenly, I could breathe again. I felt renewed, and with that renewal came clarity.

Letting go isn't always easy, but it's necessary. Clarity comes not just from knowing what to keep but also from knowing when to release what no longer serves you. Sometimes, the path forward is blocked not by external obstacles but by the things we are unwilling to let go of.

To my son: Learn to let go. It's not a sign of failure; it's a step toward freedom. Letting go clears your path and allows new possibilities to emerge. Be willing to release what no longer serves your growth.

Embracing Simplicity

"Clarity thrives in simplicity; complexity breeds confusion."

In a world obsessed with multitasking, achievement, and complexity, simplicity is often overlooked. But I've learned that the clearest thinking comes when you strip away the unnecessary and focus on what truly matters.

I remember a time when I was overly complicated in everything. I thought that success required juggling multiple priorities at once. But the more I took on, the more scattered my efforts became. I was busy, but I wasn't productive. It wasn't until I started simplifying my life—reducing commitments, prioritizing goals, and focusing on one thing at a time—that I began to experience real progress.

Simplicity isn't about doing less; it's about doing what matters most. By focusing on fewer things with greater attention, you gain clarity and direction.

To my son: Don't confuse busyness with productivity. Simplify your life by focusing on what truly matters. You'll find that when you focus on fewer things with greater clarity, your progress will be more meaningful.

The Courage to Question

"The clearest mind is the one that dares to ask why."

Clarity doesn't come from knowing all the answers; it comes from asking the right questions. The ability to challenge assumptions, question norms, and seek deeper truths is what separates clear thinkers from the rest.

I once worked on a project where everyone seemed to agree on the direction we should take. The consensus was so strong that I almost didn't question it. But something didn't sit right with me. Instead of just going along with the group, I asked questions—why this approach? What are we overlooking? Those questions uncovered a critical flaw that could have derailed the entire project.

To my son: Never stop asking questions. Curiosity is the key to clarity, and clarity is the key to wisdom. Always challenge assumptions, look beyond the obvious, and trust that asking why will always lead you to greater understanding.

Closing Reflection

"Clear thinking isn't about never making mistakes—it's about seeing those mistakes as opportunities to grow."

To my son: Train your mind, sharpen your instincts, and always seek understanding. The art of thinking clearly is one of the greatest skills you can develop, and it will guide you through even the most complex challenges life throws your way. Stay focused, stay curious, and never stop seeking clarity.

REFLECTIONS

FOR THE FUTURE

Chapter 7:

Facing Society and Reality

Facing Society and Reality

"The world isn't fair, but fairness isn't the goal. The goal is to navigate its chaos with wisdom, strength, and a sense of purpose."

Life is an ongoing negotiation with society—a tangled web of rules, expectations, and contradictions that often defy logic and reason. It is a place where the strong and opportunistic thrive while the empathetic and idealistic tend to endure. It is a world where success is often measured by arbitrary standards—wealth, status, and recognition—and where fairness is more an exception than the rule. The struggle to make sense of it all can feel exhausting as if no matter how hard we try, we are constantly at odds with a world that doesn't seem to care about what's fair or right.

For much of my life, I wrestled with this reality. At times, it felt like a losing battle—a struggle to meet the ever-rising demands of a society that seemed indifferent to my efforts, values, or needs. There were moments when the weight of society's expectations felt unbearable when I was certain that I would be crushed by the unrelenting pressures. But despite the hardship, I always found a way to rise again—not by fighting the world head-on, but by learning how to navigate its currents without losing myself in the process.

Through years of experience, I have come to understand that life is rarely fair, but that doesn't mean we are powerless. Our goal is not to bend the world to our will or to demand justice from a system that is inherently unjust. The goal is to find a way to navigate the chaos with wisdom, strength, and a sense of purpose. The world may not always give us what we deserve, but it gives us an opportunity to decide how we respond to its challenges. It is not about winning but about learning how to persevere and thrive, no matter the circumstances.

To my son: You will face a world that demands much from you and gives little in return. But if you maintain clarity of mind, resilience in your heart, and integrity in your actions, you will be able to thrive in it without letting it define who you are or how you see yourself. Remember that your power lies not in controlling the world but in controlling your response to it.

The Illusion of Fairness

"The world owes you nothing. The sooner you accept this, the freer you'll be."

As a child, I believed the world was fundamentally fair. I was convinced that if I worked hard, followed the rules, and treated others with respect, I would receive what I deserved in return. I believed that fairness was something to be expected, an unspoken law of nature. But the reality of life quickly shattered that illusion.

I recall one incident early in my career that left a lasting mark on me. I had poured my heart and soul into a project—working late nights, sacrificing time with friends and family, and pushing my limits to deliver something exceptional. But in the end, someone else took credit for my work. It was a painful betrayal that cut deep, leaving me frustrated and bitter. The injustice stung for weeks, and I couldn't let go of the anger I felt. But as I stewed in my resentment, I realized that holding onto this anger would change nothing. It wouldn't give me credit for my work, nor would it change the outcome of the situation. It only held me back from moving forward.

It was at that moment that I began to understand a powerful truth: fairness is not a guarantee—it is a luxury. The world doesn't operate according to a moral code or a system of justice; it operates according to power, connections, and timing. There are no guarantees that doing the right thing will result in the right outcome. In fact, often, it will not. Accepting this truth was freeing—it allowed me to stop expecting fairness and to focus instead on what I could control: my actions, my attitudes, and my responses to life's injustices.

To my son: Life is not fair, and it never will be. The sooner you accept that the sooner you will free yourself from the weight of unrealistic expectations. Don't waste your time chasing fairness or nursing grudges against an unfair world. Instead, focus on what you can control—your own choices and the way you respond to life's challenges. When you stop expecting the world to treat you fairly, you free yourself to create your own path to fulfillment.

The Masks We Wear

"In a world that demands conformity, authenticity becomes an act of rebellion."

In society, we are often asked—or pressured—to wear masks. We are told to hide parts of ourselves that don't fit into the molds that the world expects of us. Whether it's the pressure to appear confident when we feel insecure or to adopt values and opinions that aren't truly ours, society often demands that we perform roles that don't reflect who we really are. Over the years, I have worn many masks myself, each one a compromise between who I truly wanted to be and who I felt the world expected me to be.

At first, wearing these masks seemed harmless. They allowed me to fit in, to gain acceptance, and to avoid rejection. But as time went on, I realized that the more masks I wore, the further I drifted from my true self. I achieved success, but it felt hollow. The applause of others could never fill the emptiness I felt inside. I was proud of what I had accomplished, but I was no longer sure of who I had become. I was living according to others' expectations rather than my own values and desires.

It took me years to realize that authenticity isn't just a luxury—it's a necessity. Living authentically is not about rejecting the expectations of society entirely but rather finding ways to stay true to yourself while also navigating the pressures of the world. It means honoring your values and your beliefs, even when doing so might make you unpopular or uncomfortable. Authenticity requires the courage to be vulnerable and show the world who you truly are without fear of judgment.

To my son: The world will try to shape you into something you're not. It will pressure you to wear masks that hide who you really are. Wear the masks you must get by, but never forget the face beneath them. Authenticity is not just a moral choice—it's a source of strength. It will ground you in a world that thrives on pretense and allow you to find peace in the face of all the noise. Don't be afraid to stand firm in who you are, even if it means standing alone at times.

Thriving in Complexity

"The world is neither black nor white—it's a kaleidoscope of contradictions. Embrace the complexity, and you'll find your place within it."

Life is full of paradoxes and contradictions. It's easy to assume that the world is a simple matter of right versus wrong, success versus failure, good versus bad. But the more you experience, the more you realize that life is far more complex than these binary oppositions. The same people who praise you for your strengths may resent you for them. The same system that rewards hard work may punish independence. Navigating these contradictions requires adaptability, humility, and the ability to see the bigger picture.

I once believed that success meant winning at all costs—that being the best, beating the competition, and claiming the top spot was the ultimate goal. But as I climbed higher, I realized that the cost was often too great. I had to sacrifice relationships, compromise my integrity, and lose my sense of self to achieve what I thought was success. I began to see that success doesn't always come in the form of victory—it comes in the form of balance. It is about knowing when to push and when to yield, when to compete and when to collaborate when to speak and when to listen.

Thriving in a complex world is not about mastering the world itself; it's about mastering yourself within it. The key is learning how to navigate life's contradictions without losing your sense of purpose or direction. It's about recognizing the fluid nature of life and being able to adapt, grow, and evolve as you move through its complexities.

To my son: Life is not black and white—it is full of contradictions. Don't fear these contradictions; embrace them. They are not obstacles—they are opportunities for growth, learning, and resilience. When you learn to accept the complexity of life and navigate it with wisdom, you will find your place in the world. Success doesn't lie in having all the answers—it lies in knowing how to thrive despite the questions.

The Power of Adaptability

"Survival belongs not to the strongest, but to the most adaptable."

Adaptability is often misunderstood as a sign of weakness. People tend to view it as a lack of conviction or a failure to stand firm in one's beliefs. But in truth, adaptability is one of the most important skills you can develop. Life is constantly changing, and the ability to pivot and adjust your course when things don't go as planned is what separates those who thrive from those who merely survive.

There have been many times in my life when my initial plans fell apart. I've faced job losses, broken relationships, and personal setbacks that seemed insurmountable at the time. In those moments, my natural instinct was to cling to the familiar, to resist change. But over time, I realized that resisting change only made the pain worse. The key was to be flexible, to adapt, and to find new solutions when the old ones no longer worked. It was through this adaptability that I turned setbacks into stepping stones and failures into opportunities for growth.

To my son: Be adaptable but never rootless. Change when you must, but always hold onto the core values and principles that define you. Flexibility without a foundation is chaos, but adaptability with purpose is strength. Life will force you to adapt again and again; don't resist the change, but rather embrace it as a tool for growth. Adaptability isn't about abandoning your beliefs—it's about staying true to your core while finding new ways to navigate the world around you.

Navigating Power and Privilege

"Understand the dynamics of power, but don't let them define your worth."

In society, there are structures of power that shape nearly every interaction, relationship, and opportunity. These structures are built upon hierarchies of wealth, status, race, education, and privilege. Whether we like it or not, we are all positioned somewhere within these hierarchies, and our place often determines how we are treated, what we are given access to, and how others perceive our value.

Growing up, I didn't fully understand the complexities of power or how it operated in the world around me. I thought that success was purely a matter of hard work, personal merit, and perseverance. But as I moved through the world and experienced its realities more deeply, I realized that success is often tied to power—the power of who you know, where you come from, and what resources you have access to.

I've seen firsthand how power can be misused. People in positions of authority often wield their power for personal gain, using it to exploit others, suppress dissent, or maintain control. I've witnessed this in the workplace, in politics, and even in personal relationships—where the powerful use their influence to diminish others and elevate themselves. The damage that comes from the abuse of power can be profound and long-lasting, and it often leaves people feeling helpless, marginalized, or invisible.

But I've also seen power used for good. There are those who understand that power is not an end in itself but a tool for creating positive change. These individuals use their influence to uplift others, create opportunities, and amplify voices that have been silenced. They understand that true power is not about domination but about empowering others. True leaders are not those who sit at the top of the pyramid—they are those who build and support the pyramid, helping others to rise along with them.

Through these experiences, I learned that while you cannot always change the structures of power, you do have the ability to choose how you engage with them. Power, in its essence, is neutral. It is neither good nor bad until it is used. How you choose to use your influence in the world will define your legacy. You can choose to exploit it, to bend it to your will for personal gain, or you can choose to use it to bring about positive change. The key is to understand power for what it truly is—a tool—and to wield it wisely, with integrity.

To my son: As you move through the world, you will encounter the dynamics of power and privilege. Recognize that these forces exist, but never let them define your worth. You are not your position in the hierarchy, and you are not defined by the privileges or lack thereof that you are born into. Power can be a tool for good, but only if it is used to lift others, not to keep them down. You will have the ability to choose how you engage with power—whether you use it to empower or to dominate. Use your influence wisely. True power comes not from control but from the ability to empower those around you.

Finding Your Voice

"In a world full of noise, the courage to speak your truth is revolutionary."

In today's world, we are constantly bombarded with messages—some from the media, some from peers, and many from society itself. The noise of expectations, judgments, and opinions can be deafening. It's easy to get lost in the cacophony, to lose your sense of self in the effort to fit in or to please others. Society values conformity, and often, the loudest voices are the ones that command the most attention. But amidst the noise, it is those who have the courage to speak their own truth who stand out.

There was a time in my life when I was afraid to speak up. I worried about the consequences of voicing my opinion, particularly if it went against the grain or challenged the status quo. I was more concerned with fitting in and keeping the peace than with being true to myself. But the more I kept silent, the more I felt disconnected from who I truly was. The fear of being misunderstood or rejected silenced me, and I began to lose my sense of identity. I let others dictate the narrative of my life, and as a result, I missed opportunities to assert my values and carve out my own place in the world.

It wasn't until I learned to trust my own voice that I began to reclaim my power. Speaking up for myself, for my values, and for what I believed in became an act of defiance in a world that often values silence or obedience. It wasn't easy—it's never easy to stand apart from the crowd—but over time, I learned that the only way to live authentically is to speak your truth, regardless of how it may be received.

Finding your voice is not just about talking—it's about being heard. It's about asserting your beliefs and your boundaries and taking ownership of your own story. It's about trusting that your ideas, your values, and your perspective matter, even when they are in contrast to what the world expects or wants. It takes courage to speak up, especially when you feel like the world is pressuring you to stay silent, but it is the only way to truly live with integrity.

To my son: In a world that constantly tries to tell you who to be and what to believe, never forget the power of your own voice. Don't let fear keep you silent, for your voice matters. It is your truth that will guide you, and your words can create change. Use your voice to advocate for yourself, to uplift others, and to stand firm in your convictions. You will encounter many who try to drown you out or silence your ideas but trust that your voice has the power to create ripples of change. Speak your truth, even when it feels difficult. The world needs your voice, just as it needs the voices of all those who are willing to speak out for justice, for kindness, and for the things that matter.

Building a Legacy in an Imperfect World

"The world may not change for you, but you can change your corner of it."

We live in an imperfect world—one filled with inequality, injustice, and countless challenges. It is easy to feel overwhelmed by the magnitude of these issues and to believe that there is little we can do to make a difference. After all, the problems of the world are vast, and we are just individuals in a sea of humanity. But I have learned that the true measure of a life well-lived is not about solving all of the world's problems—it is about how much you give of yourself to make your corner of the world a better place.

You don't have to change the entire world to leave a legacy. Sometimes, making a difference means showing up for the people around you. It means being kind when kindness is rare, offering a helping hand when others need it most, and standing firm in your convictions when others waver. It means using your life, your time, and your talents to lift up others and to make the world a better place in whatever way you can.

In my life, I've tried to focus not on the things I cannot change but on the small, meaningful actions that I can take to impact those around me. I have found that it is often the smallest acts of kindness, the quiet moments of compassion, and the decisions to do the right thing, even when it is difficult, that leave the most lasting impression. A legacy is not built in grand gestures or monumental achievements—it is built in the way you live your life every day, in the choices you make, and in the way you treat others.

To my son: Don't be discouraged by the imperfections of the world. Instead, see them as invitations to act. When you see something that is wrong, do something about it. When you see an opportunity to help, take it. Leave your mark by making the world a better place in whatever way you can. Your legacy will not be defined by the world—it will be defined by the way you choose to engage with it. You may not be able to change everything, but you can change your corner of the world, and in doing so, you will create a ripple effect that will continue long after you are gone.

Closing Reflection

"The world will challenge you, frustrate you, and, at times, break your heart. But it will also teach you, inspire you, and show you the beauty of resilience."

Life is full of challenges, both big and small. There will be times when the world feels like an overwhelming force, pushing you down, testing your limits, and breaking your heart. You will encounter failures, disappointments, and moments of despair. But it is in those moments of struggle that you will learn the true depth of your strength and resilience.

The world may not always give you what you want, and it may not be fair. But it is in those moments of hardship that you will discover what truly matters: your ability to rise again, to keep moving forward, and to make the most of the opportunities you have. It will teach you how to find purpose even in pain, how to grow through adversity, and how to become a better person as a result.

To my son: Face the world with courage, knowing that it will test you, frustrate you, and sometimes break your heart. But also know that it will teach you, inspire you, and show you the beauty of resilience. Never stop striving to make the world a better place—not for recognition, but because it is the right thing to do. Keep your head high, your heart open, and your purpose clear. And remember, you are not alone in this journey—there are many others walking the same path, and together, we can make the world a better place.

Chapter 8:

Personal Growth and Relationships

Personal Growth and Relationships

"Growth begins within, but it flourishes in the connections we make with others. To know yourself is to grow, but to truly thrive, you must learn to love, to trust, and to share your journey."

Personal growth and meaningful relationships are intricately connected. They are not separate pursuits but intertwined aspects of a fulfilling life. The more you grow as an individual, the more you have to offer to those around you. And the deeper your relationships, the greater the opportunities you have to learn, grow, and evolve.

For many years, I believed that growth was a solitary journey—a matter of self-improvement and achievement. I measured my progress by what I accomplished alone, by what I could prove to the world. However, over time, I realized that the depth of my personal growth is directly tied to the relationships I cultivate and the ways in which I share my experiences with others. True growth isn't just about what you achieve in isolation; it's about building connections that nourish and challenge you and sharing those moments with people who truly matter.

The Foundation of Self-Awareness

"You cannot connect with others until you've truly connected with yourself."

Personal growth begins with a foundation of self-awareness. Without it, you are like a ship lost at sea, unable to navigate the waves of life because you lack a clear sense of direction. Self-awareness is the key to understanding who you truly are—the essence of your values, strengths, weaknesses, fears, and desires. Until you know yourself, you cannot truly connect with others because connection requires vulnerability and authenticity.

I once thought I knew myself. I prided myself on my achievements and the self-discipline I had cultivated. I believed that these external markers of success proved my self-awareness. But the more I reflected, the more I realized that I had been running from parts of myself—parts that were uncomfortable to confront. My fears, my insecurities, and my deep need for validation were shadows that I had kept hidden from view. It wasn't until I took the time to face these aspects of myself head-on, to embrace them and understand them, that I truly began to grow.

To my son: take the time to get to know yourself. Don't rush past the parts of you that are hard to face. Reflect on who you are, what you value, and what you truly want out of life. Growth begins when you stop running from yourself and start understanding who you really are. Self-awareness is the foundation upon which all relationships and achievements are built. It will guide you through life, helping you make choices that align with your true self.

Learning from Others

"Every person you meet has something to teach you—if you're willing to listen."

While personal growth is an internal process, it doesn't happen in isolation. The people around you—your friends, family, mentors, and even strangers—are powerful mirrors. They reflect parts of yourself that you might not see otherwise, and they provide opportunities for learning and growth that you cannot achieve alone.

I once had a mentor who was the complete opposite of me. I was impulsive, reactive, and always in a rush. My mentor, on the other hand, was calm, measured, and took time to think before acting. Initially, I dismissed their approach, convinced that my way was better. But as time passed, I began to realize just how much I could learn from their perspective. Their patience and thoughtful approach to problem-solving challenged me to slow down and reflect before reacting.

This relationship taught me one of the most valuable lessons I've learned: that growth is often found in the example of others. By surrounding yourself with people who challenge you, inspire you, and offer different viewpoints, you expand your own understanding of the world. It's not enough to listen to what others say—pay attention to how they live, how they approach life's challenges, and how they handle adversity.

To my son: surround yourself with people who inspire you, who challenge your thinking, and who push you to be better. Be open to learning from others—not just through their words, but by observing how they live. Growth often comes when you step outside of your comfort zone and are willing to learn from those who see the world differently than you do. Wisdom comes when you're open to other perspectives.

Building Deep Connections

"A meaningful life is measured not by what you achieve but by the connections you create."

Relationships are the heartbeat of life. They are the foundation on which we build our sense of purpose, our happiness, and our sense of belonging. Without deep, meaningful relationships, success feels hollow, and personal growth becomes a lonely pursuit. But building those relationships takes time, effort, vulnerability, and a willingness to invest in others.

There was a time in my life when I believed that achievements—titles, promotions, and recognition—were the keys to fulfillment. I prioritized work and external success over relationships, believing that if I just achieved more, I would feel more complete. But as I ticked off my list of accomplishments, I realized something was missing. Success didn't bring the lasting fulfillment I had expected. What I lacked was a meaningful connection.

It wasn't until I began to prioritize relationships— spending quality time with family and friends being present in their lives—that I began to feel a deeper sense of purpose. Relationships are not just about shared experiences; they are about mutual support, trust, and vulnerability. They enrich your life in ways that success cannot.

To my son: don't neglect the people who matter most. Life is not just about what you achieve—it's about the people you share it with. Relationships require care, patience, and effort, but they are worth every moment. The love and support you receive from those closest to you will carry you further than any trophy or title ever could.

Growing Through Adversity

"Adversity doesn't just test your strength—it reveals your potential for growth."

Some of the most profound growth in my life has come during the most difficult times. Pain, failure, and loss have a way of forcing you to confront parts of yourself that you would have rather ignored. They challenge your limits, test your resilience, and reveal strengths you didn't know you had.

I remember a particularly hard period when I faced rejection on multiple fronts—professionally, personally, and socially. It felt like the world was closing in on me. I questioned my worth, my abilities, and my purpose. In the midst of that pain, I had a choice: to stay defeated or to rise and learn from the experience. The latter wasn't easy, but it was during that struggle that I discovered my resilience. I learned to adapt, to persevere, and to transform that hardship into fuel for personal growth.

To my son: do not fear adversity. It is through hardship that you will discover your true strength. The challenges you face, while painful, are opportunities to grow. They are the fire that will forge you into the person you are meant to be. Embrace the tough times because they hold the keys to your growth.

Balancing Independence and Interdependence

"Independence is important, but so is knowing when to lean on others."

There is a delicate balance between independence and interdependence. Independence is crucial—it gives you the ability to stand on your own, make decisions, and shape your own path. However, too much independence can lead to isolation, burnout, and a sense of being disconnected from others. On the other hand, too much reliance on others can stifle your growth, creating a dependence that prevents you from standing in your own power.

For much of my life, I valued independence above all else. I prided myself on my self-reliance and my ability to do everything on my own. But over time, I realized that asking for help is not a sign of weakness—it's a sign of strength. Leaning on others, building a support system, and sharing the load is essential for growth. True strength lies not in doing everything alone but in knowing when to lean on others and when to ask for support.

To my son: be independent, but don't let that independence isolate you. Learn to lean on others when you need to. True growth happens when we support and uplift each other. You don't have to do everything on your own—let others help you, and be someone they can rely on in return.

Love as a Catalyst for Growth

"Love is not just an emotion—it's a force that transforms and elevates."

Love, in all its forms—romantic, familial, or platonic—is one of the greatest catalysts for personal growth. To love is to expose yourself, to be vulnerable, and to risk experiencing pain. But love also brings joy, connection, and transformation. It is a force that can elevate you and push you to become the best version of yourself.

One of the greatest lessons I've learned about love is that it mirrors who we are. The love we give reflects our values, and the love we receive reflects how we see ourselves. Love teaches us about our strengths and weaknesses, our capacity for compassion, and our ability to connect with others. By nurturing love in your life, you nurture your growth as well.

To my son: don't shy away from love, even when it's complicated. Love will teach you more about yourself than anything else. It will help you grow, heal, and transform in ways you cannot yet understand. Love is the soil in which your personal growth can truly flourish.

The Lifelong Journey of Growth

"Growth isn't a destination—it's a lifelong journey. Every step you take is part of becoming who you are meant to be."

One of the most common myths about personal growth is that it has a finish line—a point where you've "arrived" and no longer need to grow. But the truth is growth is a lifelong journey. It never ends. Each stage of life brings new challenges, new lessons, and new opportunities to evolve. Growth is not about reaching a destination; it's about continuously evolving and becoming the person you are meant to be.

Throughout my life, I've learned that the key to lifelong growth is curiosity—the willingness to remain open to change, new ideas, and new experiences. Growth isn't linear, and it often doesn't come in the ways you expect. It's a winding road full of detours and surprises. Embrace it. Let it shape you into the person you are meant to become.

To my son: embrace the journey of growth. Don't rush toward a destination that doesn't exist. Celebrate your progress, learn from your setbacks, and always keep moving forward. Growth is the art of becoming, and it lasts a lifetime.

Closing Reflection

"The greatest gift you can give yourself is the commitment to grow, and the greatest gift you can give others is the love that growth inspires."

To my son: nurture your mind, your heart, and your relationships. Life is richer when you grow, not just for yourself but for the people you care about. Through the connections you build, the love you share, and the growth you embrace, you can create a life filled with meaning, purpose, and joy. Together, we shape the world around us, one moment of growth at a time.

Chapter 9:

A Father's Hopes for His Son

A Father's Hopes for His Son

"A father's legacy is not the wealth he leaves behind, but the wisdom he passes on and the love he pours into his child's heart."

As I sit down to write this final chapter, my heart is full of thoughts about you—my son, my greatest gift. I find myself reflecting on the times we've shared, the growth I've seen in you, and the lessons we've learned together. Watching you stumble, then rise, has been one of the greatest privileges of my life. It is in these moments that I've come to understand that, as a father, my ultimate responsibility is not to provide wealth or possessions but to pass on wisdom and love. This book is my way of lighting a small part of your path, sharing what I've learned over the years, in hopes that it will help guide you when I am no longer there to walk beside you. Life is a labyrinth of experiences, a journey full of twists, turns, joys, and sorrows. I don't claim to have all the answers, but I do offer the lessons I've gained—hard-earned wisdom from a life lived in both shadows and light. These lessons are my gift to you, a guide for when the road ahead seems unclear, a beacon to light your way without ever dimming your own spark.

Embracing Your Authentic Self

"The world will try to shape you, but only you can decide who you'll become."

My first and most important hope for you is that you will never lose sight of who you truly are. In a world that constantly seeks to define success, to label you, to push you into molds that may not fit, your authenticity is the greatest strength you possess. The world will push you to conform, to follow the crowd, to be someone other than yourself in the pursuit of approval, status, or achievement. But none of these things will ever bring you lasting fulfillment. I spent far too many years chasing after an image of success that wasn't my own, pretending to be someone I wasn't, sacrificing my true self in the process. I believed that in order to be successful, I had to conform to expectations, but in doing so, I lost touch with what really mattered to me.

I want you to know, with all my heart, that the world doesn't need you to be perfect. It doesn't need you to fit into some idealized version of success. What it truly needs, what it will celebrate, is the real, unfiltered you. When you embrace your true self—the parts of you that make you unique, the quirks, the flaws, the passions—you will find your way. You'll attract the right people into your life, and your path will become clearer. Success, in the most profound sense, will follow.

To my son: be unapologetically you. The world doesn't need another copy of someone else. What it needs is the original, which only you can be. Never sacrifice your authenticity to please others. It is in staying true to yourself that you will find your deepest strength.

Facing Challenges with Courage

"Life will test you, but every challenge is an opportunity to grow stronger."

Life is rarely kind. It will test you. It will throw obstacles in your path, some of which will seem insurmountable. The road ahead will be filled with challenges that may shake your confidence, make you question your choices, and leave you feeling defeated. But I hope, with all my being, that when these moments come, you will face them with courage. Each challenge is not a barrier but an opportunity to grow stronger, to evolve, and to become more resilient.

When I think of resilience, I don't think of never falling. I think of all the times I stumbled, the times I thought I might not rise again, but I did. Strength isn't found in the absence of struggle—it's found in the way we rise each time we fall. In those moments when you're unsure, when doubt creeps in, I want you to remember that courage is not about never being afraid. It's about moving forward in the face of fear, about standing tall even when the path is unclear.

To my son: life's storms will come. They will shake you, test you, and make you question everything. But remember this: they will never break you if you stand firm in your belief in yourself. Stand tall in the face of adversity, and remember that each challenge is a stepping stone to becoming the person you are meant to be.

Building a Life of Meaning

"Success is hollow without purpose. Find what lights your soul and let it guide you."

I've spent much of my life chasing success—goals, achievements, titles, recognition—and for a time, I thought that these things would bring me fulfillment. But over the years, I've learned a profound truth: success without meaning is hollow. True fulfillment comes not from what you accumulate but from what you give, what you stand for, and what you believe in.

A meaningful life is not about grand accomplishments but about the quiet, everyday choices you make. It's about living in alignment with your values, doing things that bring joy to others, and finding purpose in the small moments. Whether it's through your work, your relationships, or your passions, the key is to live authentically and to pour your heart into everything you do. When you find what lights your soul on fire, you will find true success—not in the world's eyes, but in your own heart.

To my son: success is not defined by the amount of money you make or the titles you hold. It is defined by the purpose you find, the people you impact, and the joy you bring to the world. Never forget that a life lived with purpose is the only life worth living. Build a life that reflects your values, and you will find meaning even in the simplest of moments.

Nurturing Relationships with Love and Respect

"The connections you make will define the quality of your life. Nurture them with care."

As you grow older, you will come to understand that the most important things in life are not the material possessions you collect, nor the professional milestones you achieve, but the relationships you cultivate. The people you choose to surround yourself with—your family, your friends, your partners—will shape your life in ways you can't yet imagine. These relationships are your greatest source of joy, strength, and fulfillment. But they also require effort, patience, and respect.

In my own life, I've seen how important it is to surround yourself with people who uplift you, who challenge you to grow, and who love you for who you truly are. Relationships are not about perfection. They are about mutual respect, honesty, and connection. It's the small, everyday acts of kindness and love that strengthen these bonds. Invest in those who matter to you, and never take them for granted. Even in the hardest times, your relationships will be the anchor that keeps you grounded.

To my son: remember, relationships are a two-way street. Love and respect go both ways. Don't just take from those around you—give, too. Make an effort to nurture your connections with care and intention. When you do, you will find that, even in the most difficult moments, you will never truly be alone.

Leaving a Legacy of Integrity

"Your actions today shape the world you'll leave behind. Let them reflect your values."

Legacy isn't measured in the material things you leave behind. It's not about the wealth you accumulate, the possessions you gather, or the accolades you collect. True legacy is about the impact you have on the world, the lives you touch, and the values you instill in others. A life lived with integrity—honesty, kindness, compassion—leaves a ripple effect that lasts far beyond your time here.

I've seen firsthand how small acts of kindness, the quiet moments of integrity, and the decisions made with honesty and care can leave a lasting imprint on those around you. Whether it's in your family, your community, or your workplace, let your actions reflect your deepest values. Live in a way that speaks louder than words, and let your life be a testament to the goodness you wish to see in the world.

To my son: let your legacy be one of integrity. It is in how you treat others, in the decisions you make when no one is watching, and in the kindness you offer without expectation that your true legacy will be built. Leave the world better than you found it—not in what you have, but in what you give.

Embracing the Beauty of Change

"Life is ever-changing, and so are you. Embrace growth, even when it feels uncomfortable."

Change is inevitable. The world around you will change, and you will change with it. While change can often feel unsettling, it is through change that we grow. The moments of discomfort, the periods of transition, and the challenges that come with stepping into new chapters are the times when we discover who we really are.

I've learned that some of the most meaningful moments in my life came from embracing change, even when I was afraid of it. Moving to a new place, starting a new career, or letting go of the past—all of these moments held within them the seeds of growth. When I welcomed change, rather than resisting it, I discovered new strengths, new passions, and new possibilities I never could have imagined.

To my son: don't resist change. Embrace it even when it feels uncomfortable or frightening. It is through change that you will become the person you are meant to be. Let growth come naturally, even if it feels.

Finding Joy in the Journey

"Life isn't just about the destination—it's about the moments that make the journey worthwhile."

In our culture, we often place an overwhelming emphasis on reaching the next milestone, achieving the next goal, or attaining the next level of success. We live in a world that constantly tells us to keep moving forward, to strive for more, and to chase after what's next. And while there is certainly value in ambition and pursuing your dreams, I've come to realize that it's easy to get lost in the chase and forget to truly live in the present.

For much of my life, I was focused on the destination—on "what's next." I thought that once I achieved a certain goal, whether it was a career milestone, a financial target, or a personal achievement, I would find happiness and fulfillment. But what I discovered, sometimes too late, is that happiness wasn't waiting at the finish line. In fact, the moments I most cherish, the memories that stay with me, have little to do with the things I thought would bring me fulfillment.

The true treasures of life are often hidden in the simplest of moments: the spontaneous laughter shared with a friend, the warmth of family gathered around the dinner table, and the quiet beauty of a sunset on an ordinary evening. These are the things that make life rich, not the things that can be measured by achievement or success.

I've spent too many years running from one goal to the next, only to look back and realize that I missed the very moments that made life worth living. The small joys, the fleeting but precious experiences, are often overlooked when we're focused solely on the end result. We can get so caught up in our ambitions, in the pursuit of our dreams, that we forget to be present. But life is happening right now, in the moments we often overlook, and I hope you will remember to pause and savor those moments.

You don't have to wait until you've "arrived" to experience joy. Joy isn't something that's found only at the end of the road, after achieving success or crossing a finish line. It's something you create, cultivate, and experience along the way. It's in the quiet moments of connection with others, in the small acts of kindness, in the times when you're simply being present with yourself and the world around you.

As you go through life, I hope you don't rush from one chapter to the next. Take your time. Enjoy the ride. Whether you're climbing a mountain or simply walking through the day-to-day, there is beauty to be found in every step. The journey itself is the greatest reward—it's where you'll find the lessons, the memories, and the growth that truly matter.

To my son: Life is not a race to the finish line. It's a journey, a series of moments that make up the whole of your life. Don't rush through them. Don't let the pursuit of the next big thing rob you of the joys that lie in the here and now. Take time to appreciate the small moments, the ones that don't show up on a to-do list but make life worth living. Find joy in the journey itself. It is the journey that shapes you, teaches you, and leads you to where you are meant to be. Remember this: the most meaningful moments in your life will often come when you least expect them. They won't be marked by grand achievements or milestones but by the quiet, everyday moments of love, connection, and contentment. Be present in those moments. Savor them. These are the moments that make life truly worthwhile.

Closing Reflection

"No matter where life takes you, remember this: you are loved beyond measure."

As I come to the end of this book, I want you to know that I am endlessly proud of you—not because of any particular achievement or milestone, but for who you are. You are my greatest joy, my deepest inspiration, and the reason I have lived a life full of purpose and meaning. Watching you grow, discovering your own path, and becoming the person you are meant to be has been the greatest privilege of my life.

I want you to always carry with you the knowledge that you are loved—unconditionally, deeply, and without measure. Love is not about conditions or expectations; it is a constant presence, a force that will be with you through every triumph and every challenge. No matter where life takes you, no matter how far you go or what paths you choose, know that this love is unshakable. It is a foundation upon which you can always stand, a source of strength that will never fade.

I may not always be physically present as you navigate the world, but my love for you is constant, and my pride in you is unwavering. Every decision you make, every step you take, I will be cheering you on. You will never be alone, even when you feel as though you are walking through the world on your own. My love will always be with you, like a steady light in the distance, guiding you forward.

To my son: This book, these words, are my way of being with you, even when I can't be there physically. These lessons I've shared with you, the wisdom I've gathered over the years, are my gift to you. They are my way of helping you navigate the complexities of life and offering you guidance when you need it. But more than anything, I hope you will always remember that the greatest gift I can give you is my love. It is in the love I have for you that all of this wisdom comes.

I am proud of you for the person you are becoming, and I have no doubt that you will continue to grow, learn, and live a life full of meaning. Wherever your journey takes you, know that I will always be here—cheering you on, supporting you, and loving you.

You are, and will always be, my greatest blessing. This final reflection, the closing words of a father to his son, are not just about the lessons learned or the wisdom shared. They are an invitation to carry forward a legacy of love and presence, of being true to yourself and finding joy in the journey. It is a reminder that love, connection, and authenticity are what make life meaningful. No matter where life leads you, never forget that you are deeply, endlessly loved. And that, in the end, is all you need to know.

MOVING

FORWARD

Chapter 10:

Gratitude

Gratitude

"Gratitude turns what we have into enough and transforms our struggles into lessons. Moving forward begins with acknowledging where we've been."

As I sit here, reflecting on the journey that has brought me to this moment, I find myself overwhelmed by the transformative power of gratitude. It's easy to get lost in the rush of life, to chase after the next goal or milestone, and to always be focused on what we lack or what we still hope to achieve. But when we pause and truly reflect, we realize that gratitude is the key to unlocking a deeper understanding of our lives.

Gratitude for the struggles that shaped me, for the people who walked beside me, for the lessons that came not in moments of success but in the darkest hours of uncertainty. Gratitude for the quiet moments of joy reminded me, even in the midst of hardship, that life is worth living.

These words in this book are not just a reflection of what I've learned but also a tribute to the people, the moments, and the struggles that have formed me into the person I am today. It's a way for me to offer you, my son, something that can help guide you as you move forward in your own journey. No matter where you go, no matter what you face, know that you are never alone. My love, my wisdom, and my hopes for you are all woven into these pages, a constant reminder of the bond we share and the lessons I hope you carry with you.

The Gratitude for Struggles

"Every scar, every stumble, every heartbreak—they were all part of the making of who I am today."

Looking back, I see the beauty in the struggles I once dreaded. At the time, the difficulties I faced felt insurmountable. Each setback, each failure, and each moment of pain seemed like a barrier I would never be able to overcome. But now, I realize that it was through those very struggles that I grew the most. They were not just challenges to endure; they were opportunities to learn, to build resilience, and to deepen my understanding of the world.

The hardest moments in life are often the ones that shape us in the most profound ways. It's in those moments that we discover who we truly are, what we're capable of, and what we're made of. I've learned that resilience doesn't come from avoiding struggle but from leaning into it, facing it head-on, and using it as a springboard for growth.

Every scar I carry every hardship I've weathered, has taught me something invaluable. And while I wish I could protect you from the pain of life, I know that it's these very experiences that will shape you into the person you are meant to be.

To my son: Don't curse the struggles you will face. They are not obstacles to avoid—they are stepping stones. Embrace them. Learn from them. And know that, in the end, they will make you stronger than you ever imagined.

The Gratitude for Love and Connection

"The people who walk with us through life leave footprints on our hearts. Cherish them."

No one walks this journey alone. The relationships we form the people who walk beside us—whether through family, friends, mentors, or even those who challenge us—are the ones who make life meaningful. In my life, I have been blessed with many such relationships, and I am deeply grateful for them all.

It's not always easy to appreciate the people who are closest to us, especially when life gets busy or when we're going through our own struggles. But these relationships are the foundation upon which we build our lives. They remind us that we are never truly alone, even in the hardest moments. They offer us strength when we're weak, wisdom when we're lost, and love when we need it most.

I have learned that the quality of your relationships, not the quantity, is what gives life its true richness. And as much as you will contribute to these relationships, they will shape you, teaching you the value of kindness, trust, and empathy.

To my son: Value the people who stand by you. Cherish them. They are the anchors that keep you steady in the storms and the winds that push you forward in moments of doubt. Life is richer, fuller, and more meaningful when shared with those who matter most.

The Gratitude for Growth

"Growth begins with gratitude, for without it, we cannot recognize how far we've come."

Growth is not always a smooth or linear process. It is messy, uncomfortable, and often comes with growing pains. But it is through growth that we truly experience the beauty of life. As I look back on the person I was and the person I am now, I am struck by how much I've grown, not just in my career or in my accomplishments, but in my ability to handle life's challenges with grace, resilience, and perspective.

Growth is not a destination—it's an ongoing journey. And the more grateful we are for our growth, the more we can appreciate how far we've come. There are times when growth feels difficult, even painful, but those moments are the ones that push us forward, forcing us to confront our limitations and move beyond them.

To my son: Take time to reflect on how far you've come. Appreciate the progress you've made, even in the moments when it feels like you're not moving forward. Growth is not about arriving at a perfect destination—it's about continuously evolving into the best version of yourself.

Moving Forward with Forgiveness

"Forgiveness is not about erasing the past—it's about freeing yourself to move into the future."

One of the hardest lessons I've had to learn is the power of forgiveness. Not just forgiving others but forgiving myself. Holding onto grudges, resentment, or past mistakes only weighs us down. It keeps us tethered to the past, unable to fully embrace the present or look forward to the future.

Forgiveness is not easy, and it's not about excusing the wrongs done to you or forgetting the pain. It's about releasing the grip that past hurts have on your heart. It's about freeing yourself to move forward with peace, with a heart open to new possibilities. And it's something you must give not only to others but to yourself. You are human; you will make mistakes, and you will fall short at times. But the key to moving forward is to let go of the weight of guilt and regret and forgive yourself for being imperfect.

To my son: Forgiveness is freedom. Forgive others, not because they deserve it, but because you deserve peace. And most importantly, forgive yourself. Let go of what holds you back, and you'll find the strength to embrace what lies ahead.

Embracing Hope for the Future

"The road ahead is yours to walk, but you carry the wisdom of those who walked before you."

The future is full of unknowns, and that is what makes it so exciting. The path ahead is not set in stone, and that's where you have the power to shape it. But it's not just about what lies ahead—it's also about the wisdom and experiences you carry with you. You don't start from scratch. You stand on the shoulders of those who came before you, drawing strength from their lessons, their successes, and their mistakes.

While the future may seem uncertain at times, I have great hope for what lies ahead for you. With your courage, your curiosity, and the wisdom you've gained from the past, you are more than capable of walking your own path. I hope you will face each new chapter with an open heart, ready to embrace the unknown, ready to learn, to grow, and to experience all that life has to offer.

To my son: The future belongs to you. Walk boldly into it, carrying the lessons you've learned and the love you've been given. Let your story be one of strength, love, and purpose.

Finding Joy in the Present

"Gratitude is not just for what has been or what will be—it's for the here and now."

In our constant pursuit of the future, it's easy to forget the joys that are right in front of us. I've spent too much of my life chasing the next big thing, only to realize that the true treasures of life are found in the here and now. A quiet morning, a meaningful conversation, a moment of laughter with loved ones—these are the things that make life truly worth living.

Gratitude for the present moment is what anchors us in the ever-changing flow of life. When we are present, we can truly appreciate the beauty and the richness that exists in the world around us. Don't wait for the future to find happiness— take a moment to savor the joy of the present.

To my son: Don't rush through life in search of what's next. Pause, breathe, and find joy in the here and now. Life is happening right in front of you—embrace it.

Carrying the Legacy Forward

"A legacy is not what we leave behind—it's what we pass forward."

This book these lessons, are part of the legacy I hope to leave you. But my hope is that you will not only carry them with you but also build upon them. A legacy is not just about what you inherit but what you give to others.

The way you live, the example you set, the lessons you teach—these are the things that will shape the generations that follow. My legacy to you is not just my words but the way you live them. I hope that you will carry this legacy forward, not only for your own benefit but for the benefit of others as well.

To my son: Carry these lessons forward. Make them your own, and let your story be one that inspires others. Your legacy is already beginning to take shape, and it will continue to grow with every act of kindness, strength, and love.

Final Closing Reflection: A Father's Love

"No matter how far you go, no matter how high you climb, remember this: you are loved, and you are enough."

As I close this book, I want you to know that I am endlessly proud of you—not for what you've done or what you will achieve, but simply for who you are. You are my greatest joy, my deepest hope, and my most enduring legacy.

To my son: move forward with gratitude, with hope, and with the unshakable knowledge that you are capable of greatness. The world is yours—go make it better. And know this: no matter where your journey takes you, you are loved beyond measure. You are enough. Always.

Chapter 11:

A Collection of Wisdom

A Collection of Wisdom

This collection of wisdom is the result of over two decades of reflection, experience, and growth. These words weren't just written—they were lived, shaped by triumphs and failures, love and loss, and the relentless pursuit of clarity and purpose. Each quote carries a piece of my journey, a lesson learned in the crucible of life, offered now as a guide for my son and anyone seeking direction in a world that often feels chaotic.

On Character and Integrity

1. *"Be the kind of man whose actions inspire trust without needing words."*

2. *"Integrity is doing the right thing even when no one is watching."*

3. *"Your reputation is what others think of you; your character is who you are."*

4. *"A good man leaves a legacy of kindness and honor."*

5. *"Strength is measured not by how hard you hit, but by how well you protect."*

6. *"Be honest, even when the truth is hard. Lies are the chains of weakness."*

7. *"Your name is your legacy. Guard it with your actions."*

8. *"Humility is not thinking less of yourself, but thinking of yourself less."*

9. *"Courage is standing up for what's right, even when you stand alone."*

10. *"Be the man you'd admire if you were someone else."*

On Resilience and Perseverance

1. *"The strongest men aren't those who never fall, but those who always rise."*

2. *"Life's challenges are not walls—they're hurdles meant to be jumped."*

3. *"When the storm hits, remember: it's not the wind but your sails that determine your course."*

4. *"Every failure teaches a lesson; every lesson builds your strength."*

5. *"Your scars are proof that you faced battles and survived them."*

6. *"Resilience is not about avoiding pain; it's about transforming it into power."*

7. *"Keep moving forward, even if you're crawling. Progress is still progress."*

8. *"The darkest nights bring the brightest stars."*

9. *"Every setback is a setup for a greater comeback."*

10. *"Success isn't about never falling; it's about rising one more time than you fall."*

On Hard Work and Success

1. *"Work hard in silence; let your success speak for itself."*

2. *"Dreams remain dreams without action to fuel them."*

3. *"There's no shortcut to success; every step must be earned."*

4. *"Hard work beats talent when talent doesn't work hard."*

5. *"A strong work ethic is the foundation of every great achievement."*

6. *"The road to success is rarely straight, but every twist teaches you something."*

7. *"Success without sacrifice isn't success—it's luck. And luck runs out."*

8. *"Commit to excellence in everything, no matter how small the task."*

9. *"You don't have to be the best—just be better than you were yesterday."*

10. *"Success isn't measured by wealth, but by the lives you uplift along the way."*

On Relationships and Empathy

1. *"Treat others not as they deserve, but as you'd want to be treated."*

2. *"Real strength is being gentle with those who depend on you."*

3. *"Empathy is the bridge between hearts."*

4. *"Listen more than you speak. Understanding is the root of connection."*

5. *"A good friend is not the one who says the most, but the one who's there when it matters."*

6. *"Choose your friends wisely. They will shape your path more than you know."*

7. *"Forgiveness is a gift you give yourself as much as the other person."*

8. *"Never let pride stop you from saying, 'I'm sorry.'"*

9. *"Cherish the people who see your flaws and still choose to stay."*

10. *"The quality of your relationships will define the quality of your life."*

On Personal Growth

1. *"Never stop learning. A growing mind is a thriving soul."*

2. *"Invest in yourself—it's the one asset that will never fail you."*

3. *"Every day is an opportunity to become a better version of yourself."*

4. *"Mistakes aren't failures—they're lessons in disguise."*

5. *"The man who seeks to grow is never truly defeated."*

6. *"Question everything, but never lose your sense of wonder."*

7. *"Be curious—it's the spark that ignites wisdom."*

8. *"Your mind is a garden; nurture it with good thoughts."*

9. *"Success is temporary, but growth lasts forever."*

10. *"Every mountain climbed reveals a higher one ahead—keep climbing."*

On Purpose and Passion

1. *"Find what sets your soul on fire, and let it light your path."*

2. *"Purpose is not found—it's created by living with intention."*

3. *"Passion is the fuel, but discipline is the engine."*

4. *"Don't chase happiness; chase meaning. Happiness will follow."*

5. *"Your why will guide you when the how gets tough."*

6. *"The measure of a life well-lived is the passion with which it's lived."*

7. *"Your purpose doesn't have to be grand—it just has to be yours."*

8. *"Pursue what excites you, not what impresses others."*

9. *"Your talents are gifts; use them to serve others and yourself."*

10. *"Purpose gives you roots; passion gives you wings."*

On Self-Awareness and Confidence

1. *"Know yourself, and no one can tell you who you are."*

2. *"Confidence is quiet. Insecurity is loud."*

3. *"Don't measure yourself by others' standards; define your own success."*

4. *"Comparison steals joy. Focus on your own path."*

5. *"Self-awareness is the foundation of self-improvement."*

6. *"Your greatest competition is who you were yesterday."*

7. *"Trust yourself, but don't fear asking for guidance."*

8. *"Stand tall, even when the world tries to make you small."*

9. *"Be proud of your achievements, but humble in your demeanor."*

10. *"Your worth isn't determined by others—it's defined by you."*

On Facing Challenges

1. *"Adversity reveals who you truly are."*

2. *"The obstacles you face are the tools that shape you."*

3. *"Every storm you weather makes you stronger for the next."*

4. *"When you face fear, you shrink it. When you avoid it, it grows."*

5. *"The only true failure is giving up before you've tried."*

6. *"The world tests you not to break you but to build you."*

7. *"In the face of chaos, find your calm."*

8. *"The harder the climb, the greater the view."*

9. *"Don't fear struggle—it's proof that you're moving forward."*

10. *"Challenges don't block the path; they are the path."*

On-Time and Priorities

1. *"Time is your most valuable resource—spend it wisely."*

2. *"Don't waste today chasing a tomorrow that may never come."*

3. *"What you prioritize shows what you truly value."*

4. *"Learn to say no to what doesn't serve you."*

5. *"Balance isn't about doing everything—it's about doing what matters."*

6. *"Time is a currency. Invest it where it counts."*

7. *"Every moment you spend is one you'll never get back—make it meaningful."*

8. *"Busy isn't productive. Focus on what truly moves you forward."*

9. *"Don't let distractions steal your dreams."*

10. *"Cherish the little moments—they're what life is made of."*

On Legacy and Impact

1. *"Your legacy isn't what you leave behind—it's what you pass forward."*

2. *"Live in such a way that your absence is felt."*

3. *"The measure of a man is the lives he's touched."*

4. *"Success fades; impact lasts forever."*

5. *"Teach others what you've learned—it's the greatest gift you can give."*

6. *"Be remembered not for your wealth but for your kindness."*

7. *"The world is better when you contribute your unique light to it."*

8. *"Leave footprints worth following."*

9. *"Your legacy begins with the choices you make today."*

Epilogue

My Dearest Son,

As I pen these final words, my heart is filled with a symphony of emotions—pride, love, fear, and hope, all mingling in ways that words alone can barely capture. This life, with all its shadows and light, its battles and triumphs, has been a journey I now pass on to you, not with trepidation, but with the utmost confidence in who you are and the man you are becoming.

You are my greatest story, my truest legacy. Every choice I made, every trial I endured, and every moment of doubt I faced was for you—to pave a path you can walk with greater wisdom and fewer burdens. Where I faltered, I hoped to build bridges. Where I triumphed, I hoped to leave stepping stones.

The Weight of Shadows

Life has been no stranger to chaos, and the shadows I faced often felt overwhelming. They whispered doubt, echoed past mistakes, and loomed large when I felt small. But these shadows, daunting as they were, became my greatest teachers. They showed me that strength isn't the absence of fear but the willingness to confront it. They taught me that every fall is an opportunity to rise, and every scar is proof of survival.

You will face your own shadows, as we all do. When you do, remember this: shadows only exist where there is light. They are not your enemy; they are a testament to your depth, your resilience, and your capacity to overcome. Stand firm in their presence, and they will guide you toward the brilliance you carry within.

A Love Beyond Measure

If I could leave you with one certainty, it is this: you are loved beyond measure. This love is not fleeting or conditional; it is as steadfast as the sun that rises each day. My love for you has been the compass guiding my actions, the anchor in my storm, and the hope that carried me forward even in the darkest of times.

In every triumph I celebrated, I saw your future victories. In every lesson I learned, I saw the tools I hoped to pass on to you. And in every moment of doubt, I reminded myself that the legacy I leave is not one of perfection but one of perseverance.

The Journey Ahead

I cannot predict the path you will take or the trials you will face, but I know this: you are ready. You have within you the courage to face the unknown, the strength to endure the storms, and the wisdom to learn from every step of the journey.

When the road becomes unclear, trust yourself. When the weight of the world feels heavy, remember that you are not alone. The lessons of this book, the love of your father, and the strength of your spirit will always be with you.

A Legacy of Grace

Carry this legacy with pride but also with humility. Let it remind you that success is not measured by accolades but by the lives you touch and the love you share. Use your strength to lift others, your wisdom to guide them, and your heart to connect with them.

You are not bound by my mistakes nor defined by my victories. You are your own man, equipped with the tools to carve a path uniquely your own. Trust in that, and let the world see the brilliance of your light.

My Final Wish

As you step forward, know this: I am endlessly proud of you. You are more than I could have ever hoped for, and your journey will undoubtedly surpass anything I could have imagined. Wherever life takes you, carry this truth in your heart—you are loved, you are capable, and you are never alone.

The world awaits you, my son. Walk into it boldly, and may your journey be one of purpose, growth, and love.

With all my heart,

Your Father

The End